" YO, LITTLE BROTHER ..."

BASIC RULES OF SURVIVAL FOR YOUNG AFRICAN AMERICAN MALES

By
Anthony C. Davis
and
Jeffrey W. Jackson

African American
IMAGES

Chicago, Illinois

CONTENTS

iii

FOREWORD

This is a powerful work. It refutes the idea that we cannot reach our youth or that we must resign ourselves to the nihilism that is spoken and written about by so many contemporary commentators on African American youth.

When we consider the fact that the work of the Africans during the period of the Great Enslavement was devoted to surviving until the time of victory, we know something of the resilience that is in our young people. They are the children of the ones who would not be killed. They have demonstrated ways of being victorious and noble. The authors of this book have made a major contribution to the ultimate victory of our youth over the anomie, crime, lack of consciousness, and mental slavery that exist in our cities.

Rites of passage ceremonies, African holidays, African American studies, naming ceremonies, and cultural interventions through religion and art are all ways to assist our youth. Let us begin the work set out in this book and may the ancestors smile upon the deeds we do to keep the strong young people coming and winning. Hotep.

Molefi Kete Asante
Professor, Africology
Temple University

ACKNOWLEDGEMENTS

We'd like to thank our wives Denys and Kim. They told us to hang in there after our agent quit, and some of the mainstream publishing companies thought our work was too controversial to market. We would like to give a special thanks to all of the people who let us pick their brains: Dr. Molefi K. Asante, African American Studies, Department of Temple University; Dr. Jawanza Kunjufu of African American Images; The Reverend Bill Gray of the United Negro College Fund; Professor Arnold Rampersad of Princeton University; Earl Graves of Black Enterprise Magazine; Dr. Teta Banks of the Martin Luther King Center for Non-Violence; author Malcolm Kelly; Pennsylvania State Trooper David Smalls Jr.; Antonio Alphonse of BEBASHI (Blacks Educating Blacks about Sexual Health Issues); Barnnett Wright of the Philadelphia Tribune; author Nathan McCall; Sergeant Robert Michaels of the United States Marine Corps; Dr. Maulana Karenga, Chairman, Department of African American Studies, University of California, Long Beach; Dr. Winston Collins, Casimer Hylton, M.D.; Dr. S. A. Webster, D.O.; Professor Sherman Patrick, Master of Human Services, Lincoln University; and Dr. Szabi Ishtal Zee, Acting Chair, MHS, Lincoln University. A big thank you to Sandy Moore, the first person who thought our idea was serious enough to type. Thank you Alicia Woods for editing our many mistakes. An extra special thanks to Shana Peterson-Bayard who was able to bring our jumbled computer disks, handwritten papers, and scribbled ideas on scraps of paper into something coherent. Thank you to Sheila Atkins for your typing. We'd also like to thank all of the people at African American Images for giving two unknown brothers a break.

STREET SMARTS

YO, LITTLE BROTHER

Keep your hands out of your pockets when in stores.
Dateline NBC did a program that showed how young African American men are often followed around in stores by personnel. Most Black men have experienced this type of racism. Sometimes it isn't subtle. Store personnel can be blatantly unapologetic as they follow you from one section of the store to another. Apparently, they expect Black males to steal.

Arnold Rampersand, Professor of African American Studies at Princeton University, says there was a time when jewelry store owners would refuse to buzz Black people into their stores, and discrimination persists to this day. Rampersand says, "As a Black university professor living in a wealthy, predominantly White New Jersey town, a visit to almost any of the local shops is as likely as not to end in some degree of personal humiliation – from the chilly reception intonated to communicate the idea that one is not wanted on the premises to downright rudeness by the salespeople."

You can save yourself some scrutiny if you keep your hands out of your pockets, and don't spend time looking over your shoulder. Be sure to have some money in your pocket. Don't even think about shoplifting. If you get caught, even if you get a break, you'll probably end up paying about 10 times the cost of the merchandise in fines.

Always let someone know where you are going.

Your family needs to know where you are in case of an emergency. Always be accessible. If you can't get home before curfew, call home. Your family will be grateful.

Leave phone numbers, names, or addresses of where you are going if you plan to leave the neighborhood.

If you are involved in any afterschool programs, make sure your family has the phone number of the building and/or adult in charge. If you play a sport, be sure your parents have your coach's number.

Don't wander the streets without a destination.

If the cops ask you where you are going, you'd better have a concrete answer. Don't say, "Nowhere." Don't say, "I don't know." Don't say, "just hanging out." These answers will arouse suspicion. You don't want to be seen as a person with idle time. Guys with time on their hands, guys who are hanging out, guys who can't account for their time are prime suspects for police line-ups.

Get to wherever you are going and have a good time. Wandering the streets with nowhere to go is a major contribution to the high homicide rate. Time on your hands with nothing to do will get you into some serious trouble. Find something legal and fun to do, then get to it.

Never carry a weapon.

There's an old saying that goes, "If you hang a gun on a wall in Act I of a play, you'll use it by Act III." Carrying a gun will guarantee your getting sent to jail.

There are too many guns on the streets, and the authorities want to remove them. If you are caught with one, they will remove you, too.

According to FBI statistics, armed robberies, armed burglaries, and armed assaults are on the rise in America. Police are being pressured to do something about these crimes. Laws have been passed to stiffen penalties for crimes with guns. So, if you have a gun, your best bet is to get rid of it.

Don't come out of the house with a B.B. gun, air rifle, or even a toy gun. From a distance, toys can easily be mistaken for the real thing.

Unless you are a celebrity who can dish out big bucks for a good lawyer, I'd advise you to leave the guns alone. Those who live by the gun die by the gun.

Don't carry painting implements.

There is no reason for you to carry things like spray paint or markers. This will only tempt you to tag-up (write on) someone else's property. Leave other people's things alone.

You may think that graffiti is art, but when you do it without permission, it's vandalism. It makes neighborhoods look trashy, brings down property values, and inspires others to create more vandalism.

If someone catches you writing on their property, the results could be most unpleasant. Just think what you would do if you caught someone writing on your house.

If you get caught carrying markers or cans of spray paint, you will look like a graffiti suspect. If you have one of those graffiti portfolios known as a "tag book," don't carry it around outside.

If you must write on some walls, ask your parents if you can do it in the basement.

Be careful with your eyes.

In the not too distant past, Black men who stared at White women were accused of "reckless eyeballing." This could get you hurt or killed.

In the old neighborhood, staring was called "grittin'," as in "Who are you grittin' on?" When you heard that remark at a party, you knew it was time to move on.

We have a history of *not* looking people in the eyes. Sometimes there was a good reason, but today, to *not* look a person in the eyes suggests fear, a lack of confidence, or even lying.

Always look a person in the eyes when you meet them. Young African American males seem to have a problem with this. You must overcome this problem.

Don't roll your eyes when things aren't going your way. Rolling your eyes at a teacher could get you an F. Rolling your eyes at your parents could get you slapped. Rolling your eyes at a cop could land you behind bars, so don't do it.

Be careful when looking at another guy's woman. Don't stare or ogle. This is the reason behind many arguments and fights. Many altercations begin with, "What are you looking at?" Know when to look and when to look away.

7

Don't worry about fighting fair.

Avoid fighting if at all possible. There are times, however, when a fight can't be avoided. If you have already tried to talk your way out of a fight and there is no way around it, then fight as hard and as dirty as possible.

When Mike Tyson bit Evander Holyfield's ear in the ring, it was wrong. On the streets, anything goes. Head butting, biting, scratching, kneeing, kicking, eye poking, spitting, throwing low blows, and sucker punches are what you should give to people who want to harm you.

There's no referee. No one is getting paid to fight. There is no ring, no commission, no rules, only you doing whatever it takes to get someone to leave you alone. If any of these tactics work, don't hurt the person any further. Just walk away. Like Malcolm X said, "Defend yourself by any means necessary."

Don't fight unless provoked.

Fighting is for people who have failed at words. You don't have to be a sissy. You don't have to let anyone chump you. Just keep your hands to yourself.

In the old neighborhood we used to say, "Don't start no mess, won't be no mess." Defend yourself at all costs, but never be the instigator.

Don't box in the streets. Horsing around leads to fights. You start out slap boxing, then someone feels they were hit too hard and the fight is on. If you want to box, join a gym.

Following most of the rules in this book will keep you out of fights. There's enough Black-on-Black crime in America. Don't add to it.

If you are confronted by a gang, run. You should never try to fight more than one person. Don't become a statistic.

Knowing how to fight can be a great asset in your life. Knowing *when* to fight can be even greater.

Don't run at night unless being chased.

Running at night is a good way to attract attention to yourself. If the cops see you running at night, you will probably be stopped and questioned. If anything illegal happens nearby, automatically you will be a suspect.

There aren't many good reasons for a young Black man to be running after dark. If you feel the need to run, do it during the day time, or get yourself a treadmill. Go to a track or join a gym.

Even if you are late for curfew, don't run home at night if you can help it. You don't want to be mistaken for a criminal.

Don't run to fights.

The biggest problem I (Anthony) had with breaking up high school lunchroom fights was trying to get through crowds of rabid spectators. Often I was hit with a fist or flying debris. Not only would the fighters get in trouble, but the spectators too. Spectators often suffer in the long-run from cuts, scrapes, bruises, and broken bones that are caused by all the pushing and shoving. You should avoid the fighting territory and inform the authorities.

If I got hit, I would grab everyone in the vicinity of the punch, take them to the office, and let the cops weed out the truth.

Also, the jostling and distractions of the situation create the perfect opportunity for your pocket to get picked and your jewelry snatched. You may even get sucker punched by someone who has it out for you.

Never carry another guy's bag.

Stevie Wonder's "Living for the City" shows exactly what can happen when you carry another guy's bag. In the song, a guy from Mississippi gets off a bus in New York City. Another guy asks him to hold his bag while he runs across the street. The cops run up and catch the innocent guy with the bag. The poor, unsuspecting boy winds up doing 10 years in jail for what was in the bag.

Drug dealers often employ young boys as bag men. These juveniles are used because they lack a police record and they are willing to make a quick buck. Remember, if something sounds too good to be true, then it probably is.

You have enough baggage of your own to carry, both figuratively and literally. You are charged with carrying the hopes and dreams of your family, your community, and your people. That's a big bag for anyone.

Stay away from con games and scam artists.

P.T. Barnum was right. There is a sucker born every minute. If you don't think so, all you have to do is go downtown in any major metropolitan area and look at all of the people playing Three Card Monte. It's a game you can't possibly win, but people continue to get sucked in by it daily.

So you think you're different? You're a smart guy, you know a hustle when you see one. You watch the operator work the crowd, and the last guy he played won four or five times. You know you can do better, so you take the bait. Guess what? You've been hooked! That "player" was the operator's partner, and now you've lost your money, watch, gold chain, earrings, ring, and your personal cassette player.

All con games are predicated on one basic idea – your desire to get something for nothing. If you aren't trying to gain something for nothing, then you can't be conned.

Don't wear clothes that aren't useful.

Back in the 70's, we used to wear platform shoes and wide-legged elephant pants. We thought we were the coolest people to ever walk the face of the earth. If you told us we weren't hip, you'd better be ready to rumble.

One day, Dick Gregory came to my (Anthony) college and explained that we could never run from anyone with those shoes and pants on. He was right. Most of us were so embarrassed we put our shoes away and never wore them again.

Today, young African American males are wearing their pants low on their hips. They are wearing boots a half size too large and untied. Believe me, if a young brother and I were being chased, I'd be the one to get away. When you're wearing boots that aren't tied, they will weigh you down. You'll spend too much time and effort making sure they stay on. When your pants are halfway down your back side, there is no way you can run.

So, be careful how you dress. Be stylish, but dress like your life depends upon it, because it does. We're not just talking about running from cops. You could be chased by a gang or a dog. You may have to jump out of the way of a speeding car. Dressed like an inmate, however, you don't stand a chance.

Don't flash jewelry.

If you are going to wear jewelry, try not to make it too flashy or ostentatious. The jewelry that you wear to attract the opposite sex is the same jewelry that will attract the thugs, thieves, and rip-off artists.

Be careful, especially if you are on public transportation and someone asks you for the time. Don't hike up your sleeve to expose the entire watch. Cover the watch partially with your other hand then tell the person the time. If someone compliments your watch, say thank you and let the conversation end there. Don't tell where you bought it or who gave it to you as a gift or how much it's worth. Just give up the time and move on.

Police officers often look at teens wearing excessive jewelry as fitting a certain profile. Although they may deny it, lots of jewelry on a young person says "drug dealer" to a cop. Even if that watch was a present from Aunt Mabel, even if it is no one's business, you may be stopped and interrogated. Because of your jewelry, no matter how hard you may have worked for it, you could still be lumped together with jewelry-wearing drug dealers.

The newspapers are full of stories about people being killed over gold jewelry. Is a gold chain or ring worth your life? There's nothing wrong with wearing alternatives to gold jewelry. There are many ethnic styles of costume jewelry that won't get you killed and will still attract the opposite sex.

Better yet, develop a sense of self-worth that comes from inside. Don't rely on jewelry to make you feel important.

Don't take dangerous shortcuts home.

Don't take shortcuts through dangerous places. Crossing creeks, cutting through woods, crossing railroads tracks, and walking through gang infested neighborhoods can get you in trouble. Just because a creek is only inches deep doesn't mean you can't drown there. Railroads often have dangerous electrical hazards like the third rail and overhead cables. And walking through gang turf just to get somewhere more quickly is ridiculous. Use common sense.

Every day you hear about the body of some young Black boy or girl being found in a dark alley or abandoned building. Stories abound of young people being grabbed on dead-end streets and poorly lit roads.

Remember those 27 young Blacks who were killed in Atlanta? Wayne Williams was convicted for a few of them. Who killed the others? Be careful. You can easily be snatched, killed, and forgotten in America.

Don't bum rush the show.

Don't be a bum rusher. Back when I (Anthony) was in college, I was the king of the bum rushers. I never paid for a ticket to a movie or a concert. I would tell my friend who was standing in line to wave his ticket when I pointed back to him. As the ticket taker asked for my tickets, I pointed back to him and he would wave his tickets. When the ticket taker stepped aside, I'd run inside and blend into the crowd.

This scam worked many times until one day a rather large cop caught me. He jumped on my back, threw me to the floor, and handcuffed me. Two uniformed cops dragged me through the crowd. I could see my classmates and some pretty girls out of the corner of my eye. I could hear their comments and speculations about why they thought I was handcuffed.

I was taken to a back room. The concert started, and I was taken to jail. After sitting in a cell for an hour, the cops let my friends bail me out for $50.

My trial was held about a month later. I was found guilty and had to pay a $60 fine. When you add it up, money, a lot of wasted time and worry, and a lot of embarrassment, I should have bought an $8 ticket and enjoyed the show.

Don't trespass.

When you see a sign warning you to stay off of another person's property, stay off unless invited. People who fear you can use this as an excuse to have you arrested. People who fear you can use this as a reason to hurt you. If something negative happens and you happen to be in the vicinity, you could become a suspect. Ultimately, you will have to explain why you are on another person's property.

Often, signs tell you not to trespass for reasons of personal safety. In the summer of 1993, two boys drowned trying to swim in the City Avenue reservoir. There were huge NO TRESPASSING signs posted outside the reservoir, but the boys chose to ignore them, and they paid with their lives.

Don't talk tough to a man with a gun.

"You won't shoot me cause you're a punk!" "Go ahead, you don't have the nerve!" "I'll make you eat that gun!" "Wait here, I'm going to get my gun."

What are these statements? They are famous last words. These words will strengthen the shooter's resolve to put a bullet in you. These are the words that *break the camel's back*. These are the words that will get you shot.

If you find yourself on the business end of a gun, give up the loot. Don't use this time to show off how tough you are. It may be the last stand you ever take.

It doesn't take any heart or sense for someone to pull a trigger. Once the gun is out, close your mouth. Don't dare the gun holder to do anything. He or she could pull the trigger and be very sorry for it a second later, but by then it's too late.

They say there's a bullet with your name on it somewhere in the world. Don't request it.

Be careful who you bust.

"Bustin'," "sounding," "cracking," "screaming on," "doggin' somebody out," "playing the dozens," or talking about somebody's mom can get you a fat lip.

Think twice before you talk about another person's problems. Think three times before you talk about a person's physical handicap, because he has probably heard it all before. You don't know if your teasing for fun may be the thing that pushes him over the edge.

Young Black men can sometimes be hard to understand. The pressure of being a young Black man in America can leave you with a very short fuse. So, be careful who you tease.

Comedians on television give the misconception that "bustin'" is some sort of time honored tradition in African American neighborhoods. White students of mine (Anthony) have walked up to me and started saying things like "Your mama's so fat that..." I never let them finish the joke. I immediately cut them off, flag them down, jump into their world, and set them straight.

Don't be a bully.

If you are bigger, faster, stronger, or quicker than another person, don't use your advantage to bully him. If you are older, smarter, or more streetwise, don't use this as reason to bother somebody younger or weaker than you.

The person that you pick on may not be the person who sets you straight, but everything that you do will come back to you eventually. Ask any grown man who was a bully as a child. He is probably paying the price for his past behavior today.

Most of the bullies we grew up with are dead now. Most didn't make it to their 30s, some didn't make it to their 20s. Some are locked up long-term, and still others are like the walking dead, barely living on drugs such as crack and heroin.

Leave people the hell alone. You may think it's no big deal to take a person's lunch money or some small material objects, but what you are really taking is their pride. You may think that it's funny to slap or punch younger kids, but you can be gaining a life-long enemy.

You need all the help you can get to make it to adulthood. Don't close doors on possible allies. The ultimate irony is that you may have to ask the person you bully today for a job in the future.

All shut eye ain't sleep.

Have you ever overheard someone talking about you? Have you ever talked about a friend behind his back?

There's an old saying in Black neighborhoods that goes, "Every shut eye ain't sleep, and every goodbye ain't gone." Just because someone looks like they've fallen asleep or left the room doesn't mean they are asleep or away.

Words can hurt. Be careful how you use them. You don't want to be seen as two-faced or disloyal to your friends. A few careless words can destroy a life-long friendship.

A big man talks about ideas, a small man talks about other people.

Stay out of nuisance bars.

Nuisance bars are drinking establishments where some-thing illegal, disruptive, or destructive is always happening. This is the corner bar where people come for more than drinks and camaraderie. It's the place that you see on the evening news because someone is always getting robbed or shot there.

What is the appeal of sitting in a dark bar, especially on a sunny day? The best thing you can get there is drunk.

Now, don't get me wrong. There are plenty of good bars in the world if you are over 21 and want to get a drink, shoot some pool, watch a sporting event, or philosophize.

The worst bars are the "dives." Thieves come to dives to fence your aunt's VCR. Dives are those hole-in-the-wall joints where you can purchase any drug from weed to heroin.

Stay away from those bombed-out, burned-out, funky spots where most of the women are hookers and barflies. Don't put yourself in a position that can potentially be dan-gerous. You could easily find yourself caught in the cross-fire of someone else's argument or business deal gone bad.

If you are looking for trouble, it will find you in one of these joints. If you insist on going to these places, then you'd better learn how to duck.

These cells are for you.

One of the largest growth industries in America is the prison industry. All over America prisons are being built to house people who violate the law. Over 50 percent of the men in American prisons are Black. This should be of some concern to you. When you go to jail, that's one less Black person voting. When you go to jail, your children become someone else's responsibility. When you go to jail, the freedom that your ancestors worked so hard for is immediately taken away. When you go to jail, who will be left to love your wife or girlfriend? When you go to jail, your ability to live as a decent human being decreases.

Who do you think those cells are being built for? What are your chances of being sent to jail? How can you keep from getting locked up?

If you break the law, remember, you already have two strikes against you: Strike one, you broke the law, and strike two, you're Black. Ironically, most men in jail did not want anyone telling them what to do when they were boys. Now they spend their entire lives being told what to do.

Know your rights.

Not all cops are going to read you your rights before they arrest you. When you get to court, it will be your word against theirs. Chances are the judge will believe them, not you. Here are your rights.

The Supreme Court has decided that the Fifth and Sixth Amendments to the Constitution are on your side. The Fifth Amendment protects persons from being forced to testify against themselves. The Sixth Amendment guarantees a person the right to a lawyer. But don't expect to be told this by cops.

Whenever arrests are made, the arresting officer is supposed to read the suspect his "Miranda Rights." Ernesto A. Miranda was a warehouse worker in Phoenix, Arizona, who was convicted on charges of kidnapping and rape. Miranda confessed to the charges, his confession was used as evidence against him, and he was convicted. But Miranda was not told of his right to remain silent and had been denied the right to consult a lawyer. The Supreme Court of the United States reversed the conviction and Miranda was freed.

Here are your Miranda Rights. Memorize them and follow them if you are placed under arrest.

1. *You have the right to remain silent. Anything you say can be used against you in a court of law.* The best way to get around this is to politely tell the officers that you are innocent and don't want to say anything until you get a lawyer. After that, shut

your mouth. Don't say another word. Be polite, but refuse to answer anything.

2. *You have the right to an attorney. If you can't afford one, the court will appoint one for you.* Immediately tell the officers that you want a lawyer. At that point, all questioning is supposed to stop. Some cops will continue to ask you questions, but remember, you don't have to answer. Be polite, ask for an attorney, don't get an attitude, remain calm, and shut your mouth.

Don't panic when you hear the metal of the jail door close. Chances are, if you are innocent, you will get to talk to a lawyer soon and given a chance to make bail. Don't let fear make you start talking. Don't go for any deals or promises. Just sit tight and be smart.

Never hang in groups.

I (Anthony) used to hang out at 57th Street and Girard Avenue up in West Philly. On any given day there would be about 15 guys on that corner in front of a variety store. The corner was a convenient, central location for a lot of friends from the neighborhood to get together. There would be talk about sports, girls, politics, and current events. There was never any gang activity on that corner.

Years later I met a young lady who used to ride the bus past that corner. She said that she always wanted to check out that variety store, but never did. Why? Because she was afraid of the "gang" that hung on that corner. If she thought we were a gang, how many other fine sisters thought the same thing? How many elders thought we were a gang? Does the media portray Black youth in groups as gangs? Why is almost every youth murder "gang related?" More importantly, do the police view African American youth in groups as gangs?

DRIVING WHILE BLACK

D.W.B.

If you are Black, there's a crime that you and a few million other people of color commit daily. The crime? D.W.B., driving while Black. This is a slang term used by law enforcement people across the country. For many, it is a reason to stop people of color and perform unauthorized searches of their cars.

You don't believe it? Ask the thousands of Blacks and Latinos who have been stopped by the sheriff's department from Boston to Florida on the infamous Interstate 95 (the vast majority of drivers on Interstate 95 are White).

Many police order passengers from their cars when stopped, even if the officer has no reason to believe that they have committed a crime.

All of this seems unfair, and it is. Who said life was fair? The best thing for you to do is make sure you haven't been drinking or carrying illegal drugs.

Sometimes the police find illegal substances in people's cars, most times they don't. It's just like fishing. If you drop your line in the water enough times, you will get a bite.

In a commentary in the *Philadelphia Inquirer* (March 1996), Tracy Maclin of the Boston University Law School states, "A Flint, Michigan officer admitted he stopped the defendants for a traffic offense because there were three young Black male occupants in a car."

YO, LITTLE BROTHER

Maclin also states, "A Utah trooper said that as a result of a training seminar, whenever he observed a Latino driver, he wanted to stop the car and whenever he stopped a Latino driver, 80% of the time he requested permission to search the vehicle."

Drive carefully and don't do anything illegal.

Never get in a car unless you know who bought it.

In August 1996, five Black teenagers died in a high speed chase near the Philadelphia Art Museum. They were driving in a stolen vehicle.

Some of the parents, neighbors, and peers of these kids blamed the cops for the high speed chase. These parents denied that their kids did anything wrong. They should have read this rule.

With so many cars being stolen, ripped off, or jacked, accepting an invitation for a cruise could lead to trouble. So, before you get into the ride, be sure you know it's not a Johnny (stolen car).

Keep your license and registration out when driving.

When driving your proper credentials in plain view at all times. This will keep you from having to reach into the glove compartment or into your pockets. You don't want to be seen reaching for anything if you are stopped by the police.

If you are unfortunate enough to be stopped, be calm. Don't make any sudden moves, and follow the officer's instructions very carefully.

If you weren't doing anything wrong and your paperwork is in order, then you should be all right. The fines for not having a license, registration, or insurance are pretty high. You could also get your license revoked or suspended. Getting caught without these documents more than once can land you in a jail cell. It's cheaper to do the right thing the first time around. Failing to take care of business early will cost you more later.

Learn the Black rules of the road.

State police in Delaware have been known to use many reasons to stop motorists. Don't give them a reason to stop you.

Don't put bumper stickers with profanities on your car. Don't smoke your windows in states where they are banned.

Don't pick up hitchhikers. Don't give drug dealers a ride. Don't give rides to troublemakers. Don't drink and drive, and don't mix any drugs with wheels.

Be sure that all of your lights and signals are working. Make sure that your car is insured. Pay all of your tickets, and be sure that your license, registration, and state car inspection are up to date. If you can't account for all these things, park your car until you can.

Remember, you don't have to give consent for a search. Pennsylvania State Trooper Dave Smalls says, "Don't make any type of statement to any law enforcement agent without an attorney present. Even if you think it's something insignificant, it can still be twisted to be used against you." He also says, "Don't make any deals, like pleading guilty, out of fear, especially if you are innocent."

Know your public officials.

The Black Panthers, Malcolm X, and even the more subdued voices of protest demanded that we should be aware of the police who patrol our neighborhoods.

Thirty years later we have police officers patrolling our communities who look like we look, live on our block, and who may have even gone to school with us.

Today, we can know the people who have sworn to safeguard our communities. We must get to know these brothers and sisters, and we must let them know that we support them. They should know that we honor and respect their position and that we hold them accountable for how they treat us or how they permit their White colleagues to treat us. The many cases of police brutality that continue to be publicized demonstrate that the racist violence against African Americans continues and that we need all of our forces to combat and defeat it. The African American men and women who work within this system can be instrumental in dealing with police brutality.

It makes sense to know the cops in your community. Police officers can provide information about city services that you might need. They make good role models for yourself and your friends, and in case of emergency it's always important to be aligned with brave, strong, trained Black folks.

Do you know the police officers that patrol your streets? Do you think any of them have a genuine concern for the community? Do you know your local elected officials? You need to be involved in the politics of your neighborhood. You must know the politicians, the issues, and vote responsibly.

Don't rely on cab drivers.

If you are going out at night and you don't have a car, don't rely on cab drivers to bring you home. Cab drivers stereotype people they feel are a risk. Young men of color fit their profile, especially if you aren't wearing a suit and tie and it's dark outside.

Your chances of getting a cab at night decreases even more if you are heading for an inner city destination, or if you are part of a group.

A cab driver is very vulnerable. The back of his head is open to anyone who wants to take advantage of him. He or she sits in a very dangerous position, so he or she is going to be very careful when selecting passengers.

Every Black man I know has tales of being passed up by a cab, only to see the same driver pick up someone else down the street. It's hard to blame them. All they see on television are young Black men committing crimes. They can't tell the good guys from the thugs, the scholars from the hoods, the thinkers from the muggers, so they play it safe. They don't care about hurting your feelings. They care about living another day so that they can support their families.

If you are going out at night, arrange your own transportation and don't depend on a taxi cab. If you can get a cab, cool. If you can't get a cab, remember, it's not anything you did, it's their prejudice.

Recently, CBS correspondent Ed Bradley had to suffer this same type of embarrassment. Here's a man who is seen on television every Sunday evening on *60 Minutes*. He has name and face recognition, yet he too had to watch a cab pass him by on a busy Manhattan street. If this can happen to him, it can happen to you. Be prepared to deal with it.

In the hit Broadway musical, *Bring In Da Noise, Bring In Da Funk*, there is a scene in which different Black men are repeatedly passed by cab drivers. One of the brothers is wearing a suit and carrying a gold credit card, but they still don't pick him up. Every Black man in the audience had "been there and done that." These dancers managed to hit home with a painful message. The message is that even cabbies fear you, so don't rely on them for a ride home.

HOMIES

Don't let peer pressure get to you.

Most if not all of your friends that you have now will go in separate directions when you get older. They won't be around to feed you, raise your children, or pay your bills. You are going to be on your own one day, so you might as well start thinking for yourself now.

Don't let others bully you into anything you don't want to do. If a situation doesn't seem right, don't let anyone talk you into it. Listen to your heart. It won't lie to you.

Peer pressure is fear pressure. Don't fear that you'll look like a punk. Don't fear that you'll look like a lame. Dare to follow the beat of a different drummer. Read Jawanza Kunjufu's book, *To Be Popular or Smart: The Black Peer Group*. Like Dr. Kunjufu says, don't be afraid to achieve academically or in life because of negative peer pressure.

Avoid known troublemakers.

We all know someone who is just plain bad. Maybe it's the local hoodlum in the neighborhood or the boy in school who always gets in trouble. These troublemakers are usually charming and fun, and people like to hang with them. But, as you may already know, you can come to great harm just by being with the wrong person at the wrong time.

If you have an awareness of the realities of life, knowledge of yourself, self-acceptance, and self-love, you will avoid potential problems. Don't hang out with people who do not have your best interests at heart.

Play organized sports.

Many strategies and tactics for successful living can be learned and practiced through playing sports. Team sports, like football, basketball, soccer, and baseball provide great training grounds for learning skills like cooperation, strategic planning, goal setting, assertiveness, and versatility. The physical conditioning that is developed through training will also benefit your health.

If you don't make your school's team there are still many places to play. There are local PAL basketball and touch football leagues. There are leagues set up by schools, churches, YMCAs, neighborhood groups, the Boy Scouts, veteran groups, black fraternal organizations, and many others that are willing to help teach young brothers discipline, teamwork, and fair competition.

Support your brothers.

If your brother is trying to do something positive for himself or the community, he needs your support. Chances are he isn't going to get support from the rest of the world.

We have to get over the "crabs in the barrel" syndrome. When one crab tries to climb out of the barrel, another clamps on to keep him from making it out. We can't afford to stay in the barrel. We have to help each other out of it.

When a brother opens a store, buy from him. Take your clothes to a brother to have them cleaned. Support good brothers running for political office with your time and your vote. Correct young brothers when you see them doing something wrong. Congratulate brothers who do something right. Celebrate with those who make a positive difference. Let the brothers know that you are ready to add your shoulder to the wheel for a big push.

KEEPING THE FAITH

Tell the truth and accept the consequences.

There's an old saying that goes, "For each lie you tell, it takes five more lies to cover it." Lies are short-term solutions to the truth. Every lie that you tell will be found out sooner or later. Telling a lie is actually harder than telling the truth. When you tell the truth you don't have to remember made up details.

It's hard to tell a lie with a straight face. People have built in detectors that tell them when somebody is dishing up the B.S. If you are caught in a lie, you will lose the trust of that person you lied to.

So, don't tell your parents that you don't have homework when you do. They will find out the truth at report card time.

Don't do anything for which you are not willing to accept the consequences.

As a young Black man in America, sometimes all you have left is the truth.

Have faith in your abilities.

There is some talent in you that you have not fully developed. Find out what your hidden talents are and develop them to the fullest.

You may not know what you want to do with your life, and that's OK. But if you search your heart, you will find things to do that make you happy. When you find something, don't worry about how bad you are at it in the beginning. Stick with it.

Sure, you won't be the best rapper, dancer, musician, athlete, or whatever when you first start out the gate. But most people aren't. Did you know that Michael Jordan didn't start on his J.V. team? Did you know that Einstein failed math? Did you know the famous actor, James Earl Jones, used to stutter?

History is full of examples of people who overcame adversity and disabilities to become great. What separates the achievers from the non-achievers is faith in their abilities. There will be many people who tell you that you can't. If you believe them, you can't. If you believe in yourself, you can.

In high school, I (Anthony) played offensive guard on our football team. I only weighed 150 pounds. Everyone that I lined up against outweighed me by more than 50 pounds. I was the lightest weight lineman in the Catholic league. Guys on the other teams would laugh and make comments when they lined up against me at the beginning of the game. I could have let this discourage me, but it only made me play harder. By the end of the first couple of plays, they could see they were in for a fight. By the end of the first quarter, I had earned their respect. By the end of the season, I had made honorable mention on the All-City Team.

Wear something African.

Wearing a scarf, shirt, jacket, or tie made of kente cloth, mudcloth, or some other African-inspired patterns shows the world that you are proud to be an African American.

You can buy Africentric clothing almost anywhere in America these days. There are many stores around the country that sell African styles of clothing and accessories.

You don't have to dress African from head to toe. All you need is one Africentric item to make a cultural statement.

If you are not able to dress African at work, then show the world your pride on your own time.

Don't wait for praise.

Do your job. The reward for doing your job is that it's done. If you know you did a good job, that's all you need. Black men aren't always given credit for the good things that they do. For example, there are many Black inventors who only get mentioned during African American History Month.

Unless you are an entertainer or athlete, don't expect to receive respect for your endeavors. Smart Black men are always questioned on their credentials. Black professionals are always questioned on where they attended school.

People will not give you the benefit of the doubt. If you are a craftsman, you better do the best job that you can. If you make a mistake, you will be accused of doing "nigger business." How many times have you heard someone mention that you should get a Jewish doctor or lawyer? How many Black people look for Italian bricklayers? Why can't we call on our own people to work on our houses or cars?

Part of the reason is that we are conditioned to think we are worthless. We are constantly told that we are worthless. Our women are told we will leave them so they expect the worst from us.

So learn to live without hearing praise. Praise yourself.

Use your culture as a shield.

Western cultural concepts such as individualism, materialism, capitalism, and acquisition (i.e., getting all that you can at any cost) do not serve us. Cliches such as "I'm doing my own thing," "He who dies with the most toys wins," and "I'm getting mine," are classic Western cultural concepts. On the other hand, African philosophy upholds the good of the group over the needs of the individual. Family and extended family are viewed as the building blocks of society (communalism). Respecting and protecting the earth and environment is primary.

We need to counter harmful Western influences with positive African practices and beliefs. You need to join a rites of passage or mentoring program.

Maulana Karenga gave us the gift of the Nguzo Saba or the Seven Principles. They help guide our daily actions in a more positive direction. The seven principles are:

Unity
Self-determination
Collective Work and Responsibility
Cooperative Economics
Purpose
Creativity
Faith

There are many books, articles, videos, and people available to discuss or explain the seven principles in-depth and you should learn as much as you can about them. We should honor the principles of Kwanzaa all year round, not just during Kwanzaa, which is celebrated December 26–January 1.

A TIME TO LEARN

Learn from the mistakes of other brothers.

People often ask us how we managed to stay out of trouble growing up in the heart of Philadelphia. So many of our friends are dead, in jail, or on drugs (the living dead) that people we see from our old neighborhoods wonder how we made it. When we see someone that we have not seen in years, the first thing we do is start naming names and asking about this person we played ball with or that guy who lived down the block. Most of the guys are dead.

We tell people that we learned from other brothers' mistakes. When we saw a brother get into serious trouble, we had enough common sense to not follow that path. Of course we did our dirt. We were not saints, but we had limits. We kept our eyes open and tried not to take foolish risks. We saw what happened to brothers who used dope. We saw what happened to guys who talked trash. We saw what happened to brothers who sucked on a crack pipe. We saw how these things got brothers locked up or killed. We learned that we did not have to make these mistakes.

YO, LITTLE BROTHER

Study hard.

Education is the key to life. Once you learn something, no one can ever take it from you. Education prepares you for the future. Without education, you will have no future. You prepare for the future by what you do in the present.

Never walk into a class empty handed when homework is due. The man with excuses always gets an F. Even if your teacher has been working for only a year, he or she has probably heard every excuse imaginable.

Work on your homework with the same determination you give to memorizing lyrics to a rap tune. Study as hard as you play. Put the extra effort you would give to winning a basketball game into earning an A. Ask your teachers to give you extra credit work or tutoring on difficult subjects.

The world is hard enough for Black people with diplomas, degrees, and certificates. For those who haven't finished school, it's twice as hard.

Become computer literate.

The industrial revolution was powered by oil and the internal combustion engine, but today the information age is powered by the computer. Information is power. The computer is used in all aspects of life, from scanning in stores to flying airplanes and saving patients.

Young people easily master the latest versions of Mortal Kombat and NBA Jam, but are you just as likely to be proficient on Windows, Power Point, or the Internet? Gaining proficiency in word processing, design, and spread sheet programs—not video games—is the ticket to success and making money.

Young African American men cannot afford to be left out of cyberspace. Remember, on the Internet everyone is the same color and, like author Reginald Lewis said, *"Why should white guys have all the fun?"*

Don't cut school.

Nothing good can come from cutting class. The time wasted dodging cops, truant officers, and other adults could be spent doing something constructive. During your teen years, you should be preparing for you future.

The day that you cut class will be the day that you miss key information for the next test. When you flunk the test, you will feel embarrassed and probably want to hide your face by cutting some more. The more you cut, the more you'll fail. It's a vicious cycle.

When you look for work, employers sometimes check your school attendance records to assess your dependability. If you have to go to court, judges and prosecutors may look at your attendance record. A poor record would be one more strike against you.

If you have dropped out of school altogether, enroll in a class to get your GED. If you are thinking about dropping out, don't. There is nothing for you in the streets. Education is the only way to make it. It's the key to everything good in life.

Slaves who tried to learn were killed. Blacks who were the first to enter all White schools during the 1950s and 1960s were beat and spat upon. They knew the value of education. Keep their legacy alive by not cutting school.

Learn something about Africa.

During my 20 years as a school teacher, I (Anthony) had to constantly explain to students that Africa is a continent, not a country. Also, many young students are still under the impression that Africa is a jungle. Africa has many large cities filled with highways and hotels. It also has plains, deserts, mountains, and just about every type of land imaginable. Africa consists of 54 countries, hundreds of communities, sometimes called tribes, and more than 1,000 languages. There's enough information about Africa to keep you learning for a lifetime. Africa is the richest continent in the world, possessing the largest amount of gold, diamonds, uranium, and oil. Africa is the cradle of civilization.

When I told the young brothers about the warm welcome I received in Senegal and Gambia, they were surprised. Like many older African Americans, they believed the myth that Africans don't care for us.

Read books on Africa. See films on Africa, such as *Sankofa*. Go listen to some African music. Check out some African museums. Buy some African clothing.

Be a listener.

Know when to be quiet. When the teacher is lecturing, when your parents are talking to you, or when you are being questioned by the police, listen carefully to all instructions.

Don't say a word until you are asked to speak. Don't give more information than what is asked of you.

When you interrupt a speaker, you ruin his train of thought. You don't want anyone interrupting you, so be considerate of others.

A good listener will digest what a speaker is saying and be able to give some logical feedback. If you didn't understand what was said the first time, politely ask the speaker to repeat himself.

A wise man once said, "When two people are talking at the same time, nothing has been said." A good listener will always be able to ask an intelligent question. Don't be afraid of sounding stupid, however, if you have a question. "When in doubt, check it out." (Anon) Let this be your guide through the journey of life, young brother. By listening carefully, you will be able to separate those who will or won't help a brother.

Behave in class.

You may think that joking around in class is fun. You may think that being out of your seat is no big deal. You may think that the piece of paper you just threw at another student is just between the two of you. The reality is, every time you cause a disruption or break class rules, you force the teacher to waste precious time and energy away from her job of teaching you and preparing you for adult life. When the teacher has to use most of his time on discipline, everyone in the class suffers.

How can anyone in a class of 25 or 30 learn when three or four people are acting up? Not only are you missing the work that you need for the future, but you are making the people who want to learn miss their work too. It's a no-win situation. You are keeping other brothers from surviving. You drag all of the young Black men down with you. If you don't want to learn, at least be quiet so others can.

Read, read, read.

It doesn't really matter what you read, as long as you read. Newspapers, magazines, comics, novels, but find something to read.

Young men in our neighborhood sometimes think that only sissies read comic books. I (Anthony) learned the word "idiosyncrasies" while reading a Spider Man comic. Some feel that they don't have the time to read. Others feel it's a waste of time...but it isn't.

The more you read, the more you know. The more you know, the further you'll go. Reading is the key that will open the door of success for young Black men.

You want to be able to converse with anyone on any level. When you are well read, you can keep up with any conversation. You won't need people explaining every little detail to you.

You can add your two cents worth with an informed opinion. Reading and staying aware of current events will keep you from sounding like a fool when the conversation goes beyond the weather. Go to the library. Go to a bookstore. Find something that sparks your interest, and start reading.

Keep a paper and pen handy.

Try to keep paper and a pen on you at all times. While it is possible to use a matchbook or napkin, having a note pad or an appointment book works much better. This is a tool that has many uses from writing down addresses, appointments, ideas, rap lyrics, jokes, and, of course, that young lady's number.

Don't feed into the idea that African Americans aren't detail oriented. Many African American inventors, scientists, writers, and leaders made it big because they were able to put ideas on paper.

There are too many things that can be distracting to young African American men, so don't rely on your memory if something important needs to be written down. Don't be one of those brothers who misses out on the job opportunity, the chance to advance, scholarship, or anything else positive because he couldn't remember that phone number, fax number, box number, address, name, or whatever. There is nothing wrong with having a bad memory. It only becomes a problem when you don't write things down.

YO, LITTLE BROTHER

Learn even when you're not in school.

Don't expect to learn everything you need to know in school. There is just too much to learn in life. No teacher can give you all the information you need to live your life as a Black man in America.

You'll have to go beyond the classroom walls to get your education. You'll have to read more books than those assigned by your teachers. You'll need to read newspapers daily if you want any in-depth news. Ask questions if you want to understand things clearly.

Make the mechanic explain how he fixed your car. Ask the accountant how he did your parents' income taxes. Talk to the reverend about religion. Mark your travel route on a map. Stop and look at the way the guys are laying cement. Stop, look, ask questions, and listen.

You can learn something new every day of your life, if you are aware. There is so much you can learn for free. Keep your mind open and get ready for the flood of information.

Listen to old folk's stories.

> *"There's no such thing as an old fool, 'cause you don't get old being no fool."*
>
> —Moms Mably

We are writing this book because we want to help young Black men have healthy and happy lives. We also want to help you make it to old manhood.

The best way to find out how to live a long and healthy life is to talk to the elders. Our elders are a rich resource of wisdom and information. They can help you understand how Black people overcame adversity.

Seniors can also give you some good laughs. They have a way of making any story seem funny. Having survived many trials and tribulations, elders have learned to not take themselves or the world too seriously.

Learn how to take notes.

While teaching at Community College of Philadelphia's Learning Lab, I (Anthony) always gave students the following list of tips to help them take good notes:

1. Keep a written record for each class. When in doubt, write it down.
2. Sit where you'll be seen. Your position near or at the front will help you stay tuned in to what the instructor says in class.
3. Read in advance. Read, especially about the topics to be discussed in class.
4. Record notes systematically.
5. Use an outline format to take down notes.
6. Be alert for signals. Watch what the instructor puts on the blackboard, emphasizes, lists on a handout, pronounces as important, etc.
7. Write down examples.
8. Write down details that connect or explain.
9. Leave some blank spaces all around your notes.
10. Ask questions.
11. Take notes during discussions.
12. Take notes right up to the end of the class.
13. Review your notes right after class for accuracy. Review them again within a day and on a weekly basis thereafter.

If you follow this set of rules, you should be able to understand anything that was taught in class on any particular day. You'll prove to yourself and everyone else that young Black men can be organized and prepared.

Get involved in an extracurricular activity.

Learning from books is an extremely important part of school. The academic subjects prepare you for adult life. To be a truly well-rounded person, however, you must get involved in some of your school's extracurricular programs. Extracurricular activities give you an extra reason to come to school. It gives you a chance to be part of something that you may not have the opportunity to do later in life. Oftentimes, colleges and employers review your extra curricular activities before making their final decision.

Do you like to argue and make your point? Join the debate team.

Do you like games of strategy? Join the chess team.

If you like music, join the orchestra, jazz, or marching band, choir, or glee club.

If you like sports, get into swimming, track and field, football, baseball, basketball, bowling, golf, tennis, badminton, field hockey, soccer, or softball. Remember, basketball is not the only sport. Be an athlete or serve the team as a manager, statistician, timekeeper, or water boy.

There are language clubs, honor societies, science clubs, business clubs, and community service clubs.

Join the yearbook staff or newspaper staff. Participate in a talent show. Don't let your peers make you think these things are uncool. Keep yourself busy and out of trouble.

Learn how to work with your hands.

A man who can't fix anything will always have to pay for services when things break. Repair men don't come cheap. So learn how to fix small things before they become big problems.

Get some basic tools and a book from the library, and you can do quite a number of small repairs around your house or apartment. When you see electricians, plumbers, or carpenters working, stop and watch what they are doing. While it is important to develop your mind, it is equally important to learn how to use your hands. You become valuable when you can do both.

Use your hands to paint a house. Use them to tinker. Use them to create. Use them to build. Use them to plant. And when you learn a new skill pass it on to another brother.

UNDERSTANDING YOUR EMOTIONS

Have the courage to ask for help.

Nobody's perfect. Everyone needs help at some-time. We are born completely dependent on our parents or caretakers to satisfy our needs. Survival, life itself, can only be sustained by the help we receive from others. As we move through life, the need for help never ends, it just rises or falls according to our capabilities at any given moment.

Just as we depend on others to help us when we're babies, so, too, do others depend on us at various times. For this reason, young Black men should never be afraid to ask for help.

When running ball on the court, if the guard is bringing the ball up court and the forward has beaten the defense to the basket, the forward will not hesitate to call for the ball. What is known as an assist in basketball is the same as getting help in life to achieve a goal.

A wide receiver in football will throw up his hand to let the quarterback know he's open. That's communicating, asking for help to achieve a goal.

These sports analogies relate to games, but they apply as well to the game of life. Whether in sports or in life, knowing when to ask for help can help you achieve a goal or avoid trouble. Many men feel asking for help such as tutoring, is a sign of weakness. Put aside your pride and ask for help when you need it.

Take every positive chance you can.

The only way to advance is to sometimes take a chance. If you don't take risks, there are no rewards.

The world is full of stories of people who have risked everything to start a business, invest in a good idea, or make a career change.

On the other hand, the world is full of stories of people who blew their chance and wish they had that chance again. Then they spend their lives waiting for that chance to come around again.

Think every new idea through. Discuss your opportunities with others, then act on them.

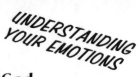

Know that your guidance counselor isn't God.

I (Anthony) went through 12 years of Catholic school. In 12th grade, my guidance counselor told me that I should apply to a community college. Actually, a two-year school had offered me a partial scholarship to play football.

He told me that my football skills wouldn't land me in a four-year school. He was probably right, but I didn't want to go to a four-year school to play football. I wanted to study.

This gentleman of poor judgment barely glanced at my above average SAT scores because he had already made an assumption about me. He didn't know that my SAT scores were higher than both of my sisters, who were in college already. I knew that some four-year school would admit me.

On my family's advice, I applied to seven different colleges on my own: Temple University, Delaware State, La Salle, University of Ohio, Central State, Wilberforce, and Hampton University. To my astonishment, I was accepted by all seven.

I never got mad at the counselor, but as each acceptance letter came in, I made sure he knew about it.

Don't accept other people's judgments about you. Take matters into your own hands. Send out your own applications. Get help from minority college recruitment organizations. Make calls to friends already in college. Do research in the library on scholarships, grants, and other financial aid programs. You are the master of your fate.

YO, LITTLE BROTHER

Don't seek revenge.

"Vengeance is mine says the Lord." Payback, get back, revenge, or whatever you want to call it is a waste of time. It involves too much looking back. It keeps you from moving ahead.

Do two wrongs make a right? No. Cut your losses and move on. Your time on this planet is too limited to worry about payback or revenge. You are a young Black man in America. That means your life expectancy is shorter than just about everyone else's in this country. Don't shorten it even more by seeking revenge.

There's an old saying that goes, "When you seek revenge dig two graves, one for your enemy and one for yourself." When you feel that someone did something wrong to you, tell them about it. Then forgive, forget, and let go.

Know yourself.

You should strive to gain as much insight into yourself as you can. The more you know about yourself, the better your chances of surviving as a Black man in America.

Knowing yourself physically, mentally, emotionally, and spiritually means identifying your needs and making plans to meet your needs in healthy, productive ways.

Know your body, your dimensions (height, weight, clothing size), and your physical abilities (speed, strength, and endurance). Learn your limitations then work to improve them.

Know your mental self. What kind of person are you? Easygoing or aggressive? Quick tempered or passive? Take an honest look at the way you think about things.

Know yourself emotionally. You should be able to identify how you are feeling at any given time.

To be a fully developed and productive human, you should be able to draw on more than just your physical self for survival and growth.

Never let another person think they know you better than you know yourself. You are a work in progress and you're capable of changing and growing. Don't be so cool that you don't know yourself.

Don't watch too much television.

The mass media in America (radio, television, newspapers, and movies) have been a major weapon in the attack against Black folks in general and young Black men in particular.

We are constantly portrayed in unfavorable and unintelligent ways on television. Today, Black people watch more television than any other group. The problem is not just negative programming, but the fact that TV watching is mindless and sedentary. It takes precious time away from other productive, meaningful pursuits.

Instead of watching TV, study your schoolwork, read, exercise, look through want ads, write a resume, plan a business, explore cyberspace, cultivate meaningful relationships, or find something to repair.

Learn to recognize the signs of depression.

Among young people, depression is often overlooked, misdiagnosed, or minimized as "growing pains" or confused immaturity. Many young Black people are depressed and don't realize it.

Depression is a serious and debilitating problem, but it can be successfully treated if it is recognized and addressed. The following are symptoms of depression:

- sad, anxious, or empty feeling that won't go away
- feeling hopeless, helpless, guilty, or worthless
- loss of interest in things which were once pleasurable, such as friends or family
- changes in sleep patterns—trouble getting to sleep, early awakening, oversleeping
- changes in eating habits (losing weight, no appetite, gaining weight)
- low energy, feeling fatigued, run down, or tired all the time
- restlessness, irritability
- trouble remembering, concentrating, or making decisions
- suicidal thoughts or attempts, preoccupation with thoughts of death.

Read and recognize the symptoms listed above. If you or a loved one is experiencing two or more symptoms, seek help.

Volunteer your time to help those less fortunate.

Helping out at a homeless shelter, senior citizens program, or youth recreation center can provide therapeutic benefits. Feeling needed and appreciated can increase your self-worth. Another benefit is that you can gain skills and experience, and volunteering is one of the best ways to move into a paying job. Volunteering can help teach you responsibility and good habits, such as punctuality, following directions, dependability, and maintaining a good attitude.

By helping other people, not only do you give of yourself, you earn good "karma" (what goes around comes around). Volunteering can help you deal with your problems; it helps take the attention off yourself. Also, selflessness (putting others ahead of yourself) and altruism (regard and devotion to the welfare of others) are qualities that will go a long way in helping to make your life feel complete.

The African American community needs all the help it can get from its young men. What are you waiting for? You are the untapped and uncounted resources that all of the forces working against us don't want to see.

When the young men—the warrior class—become a powerful force for the positive, the lives and communities of Black folks will change for the better. Malcolm, King, Douglass, Garvey, and DuBois lay down their lives for our freedom. Your ancestors are watching and waiting.

Define your own Blackness.

People will try to tell you how to be a Black man. You don't have to do anything to prove your Blackness to anyone. If you are Black, then you are Black.

You don't have to play basketball to be Black. You don't have to be a good dancer to be Black. You don't have to like Black sitcoms to be Black. If you are Black then you are. You can like any type of music you want and still be Black. You can dig country and western and still be a brother. Liking opera doesn't diminish your Blackness one bit. Folk music? Cool! Heavy metal? If that's what you like, no problem. Listen to whatever you want. It's your thing. It's all good.

If you want to watch ice hockey, skiing, swimming, or polo instead of basketball or boxing, you don't have to explain it to anyone. You're still a Black man. Sports are sports. Competition is competition. Like whatever you want to like, as long as it doesn't hurt anyone else.

When you leave your house, you are still Black in the eyes of the oppressors. As long as you aren't doing anything that will bring shame on your people, enjoy yourself.

Don't worry about people who think you are an Uncle Tom because you're pursuing an education. Only a fool would question your Blackness because you have a degree.

No one expects all White people to like the same things. Why should all Black people be expected to have the same tastes?

To be Black is more than possessing a large dosage of melanin. It means valuing your history, culture, and commitment to the liberation of African people.

Keep your hostility in check.

The angry young Black man is almost a cliche. Turn on any radio station and you will hear rappers talking about being angry. Turn on the television and you will see images of angry young men of color sneering at you from the latest music videos. Go to the movies and it's a virtual parade of brothers shooting guns, fighting, disrespecting women, and perpetuating the image of angry Black men.

Yes! We have a lot to be angry about. The fact that we are judged by the color of our skin is very hard. The fact that we fill the prisons and die at a disproportionate rate is enough to make you angry. Your schools sometimes don't give you a proper education. You are followed around in stores. People fear you. You have plenty of reasons to be angry. But don't turn your anger inward. Don't let it make you hate yourself or your people.

Use your hostilities in a positive way. Pick up a pen and paper, not a gun. Write about your concerns to your Congressman, to newspapers, to magazines, to anybody who you think will listen. Write about the things that bother you. Write about the things that are missing in your community. Write about the improvements that are needed in your community. Get together with your friends and voice your concerns. Don't complain that there is no help until after you have sent out at least 100 letters. If you don't get any help by then, send out 100 more. If you don't speak up, who will?

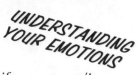

No one will ever know your problems if you aren't willing to speak up. If you hold these hostilities inside, you will become bitter. You will become a skeptic and a cynic. Sitting around complaining to your friends will do nothing for you. Your friends don't have that kind of power. They have the same problems you have.

Listen to your inner voice.

The truest, most personalized guidance you can get is the quiet voice which speaks within you. You can only hear the voice if you learn to separate the noise and clatter of everyday life from the quiet, calm voice of your inner self. This ability, like most others, can only be discovered and developed through practice—repetition.

It is the voice that warns you when something's not right. It is the voice that softly says "yes" when you make that lay-up or get that phone number. This voice of spiritual guidance is always there. Our ancestors in Africa relied on their inner voices to survive. They felt it was their ancestors serving as guardian angels.

Spend some time in silence daily. In silence you will hear your inner voice. Learn to sort out the many impulses constantly circulating in your consciousness. Above the many messages going around this or that, you will hear a steady, calm voice, usually carrying a simple message. Hear the voice. It is your inner self communicating with you. Spiritual folk might say it is the voice of the Holy Spirit, the ancestors, or the universal consciousness. Train yourself to hear it. Command the voice to speak to you in positive messages. Otherwise, it will become the voice of self-doubt—the woulda, shoulda, coulda voice.

In prayer, meditation, or just relaxed quiet, ask for positive guidance. Then listen to your inner voice as it speaks only to you.

Never trouble trouble until trouble troubles you.

You are a trouble magnet. It may sound negative, but you are. Don't look for trouble because as a Black man, it will look for you. If you know there is a possibility of trouble at a certain place, then don't go there! Go somewhere else.

The problem stems from the fact that a lot of the young brothers who commit crimes look like you. When the description comes over the police radio, it is often someone who looks like, dresses like, and has a hairstyle like you.

How do you avoid being caught up in a police sweep? Well, sometimes you can't. Often it is a matter of being in the wrong place at the wrong time. The best you can do is to avoid being in the wrong place.

In their haste to solve a crime, sometimes police will grab every man of color and sort out the height and weight difference later. If you are anywhere close to the profile, they are looking for you. Be prepared for a ride to jail. The moral of the story is, if you are a man of color, sooner or later you will be picked up, whether you did something or not. So don't have anything illegal on you when you do. Have a reason for being where you are. Make sure that you can account for all of your time.

Respect your feelings.

In the "Know yourself" rule, we discussed getting in touch with all of your many parts. In today's stress filled, high tension world, knowing how you feel, and understanding how feelings influence your actions, is important.

Feelings are important contributors to the level of enjoyment and fulfillment you get out of life. We're constantly experiencing joy, sorrow, excitement, love, worry, fear, and countless other emotions. Learn to recognize and identify your emotions. Being unaware or in denial of how we are really feeling at any given moment can lead to poor decision making. A bad decision you make today can lead to lifelong problems.

Too many young Black men get violent when emotions get out of control. A statement made in the heat of anger can cause a breakup in a close friendship or relationship. Passing up the chance to do something because you're feeling sad might cause you to miss the opportunity of a lifetime. Not asking that cute girl to a dance because of fear could leave you feeling lonely all night.

Knowing and respecting your feelings are the first steps to controlling and moderating them. Respect your feelings and learn to turn them up or down depending on the situation.

Use anger as a motivator.

"Don't worry, be happy."

—Bobby McFerrin

Hell yeah, I'm mad. Every Black person struggling to survive and be sane in today's world, or who has family struggling, or who cares about those people struggling, should be mad. Jobs are scarce, educational opportunities are limited, positive motivation is rare, emotional and psychological stressors are ever present, and hope for the future is buried beneath doubt, fear, and sadness. It's enough to piss you off, and it does. In fact, if you're not angry, you should be.

So while you have a good mad on, get up on your feet and go do something to change things. Get a pen and paper and write a letter to your Congressman or the President, or write a resume. Go get a broom and shovel and clean up the trash on your block. Go get a paintbrush and volunteer at the local community center. Go down to the corner and drop some science on the young men hanging out.

Use anger as a motivator. Rage against the machine, but not yourself, your people, or your community. You have good reason to be angry. Just be angry at the right things for the right reasons.

Anger is one of the most powerful emotions and probably the most dangerous because it is so unpredictable and difficult to control. However, anger, like fear, can be a great motivator and using it to push you into a positive action is highly empowering.

Look for your father if he's not around.

A strong sense of self is crucial to survival and sanity. Your father, if he's in your life, can help you understand who you are. If your father is not around, you should try to establish communication with him when you feel ready and are of age. I know it's a big responsibility and this relationship should have been started by your father.

The separation of the Black father from his children is a plague in our community. The pain of this separation has been enormous on children and mothers. Young people of today must try to break the cycle of despair by talking to their fathers.

Black fathers are separated from their children for a variety of reasons, and the root of the problem goes deep. If your father is not around, if you've never met him, it's quite possible that you don't know the full story behind his leaving. Maybe he has fallen in a bad way and needs your help.

If you are able to establish communication or, perhaps, get a better idea of who he is, you can learn more about yourself. You might have nothing to say to each other at first, or maybe words will come tumbling out. It doesn't matter.

If you're not able to find your father, the act of looking can help bring closure to the mystery and help heal emotional wounds. You may meet friends, relatives, or acquaintances of your father who can tell you something about him. Learn all you can about him, and use that knowledge to benefit yourself.

Never lose touch with your children.

One of the biggest threats to the psychological well-being of many Black men is the denial or lack of connection with their children.

This problem is well documented in terms of the damage that it does to the child, but the damage that occurs to the father is not discussed. The vast majority of the guys I (Jeffrey) grew up with fathered their first child before the age of 21, many before 18. Unfortunately, these young fathers were not equipped or educated to care for a child or the child's mother. The relationship, if there was one, often shattered soon after the baby's birth, sometimes before.

The young father might see his child while hanging out in the neighborhood with his boys. Mother and child may only live a few blocks away and they still have no contact. The young father may be in conscious denial, but unconsciously he never forgets his child. His basic instinct constantly reminds him that his own flesh and blood are somewhere in the world. Guys carry it around like their own dirty little secret.

This creates conflict between what the young father knows should be and the reality of the situation. The lack of contact over time becomes abandonment or denial of the child and leaves a large emotional and psychological void that affects every part of the man's life.

YO, LITTLE BROTHER

Sadly, most of my friends who lost contact with their children have had very difficult lives filled with drug addiction, crime, poverty, arrested development, and dashed hopes. The guys who have made their relationships work, at least on a parental level, are doing better. By sticking it out and maintaining some contact with their children, these guys have avoided the emotional and psychological distress that leads to drug and alcohol abuse and the despair, crime, and death that follow.

Yo, little brother, don't become a father until you become a husband and are emotionally ready to stay forever.

CROSS CULTURE

YO, LITTLE BROTHER

Don't blame all of your problems on the White man.
We've been hearing about how the CIA suppos-
edly saturated Black neighborhoods with crack.
Whether this is true or not, nobody forced anyone into smoking it. The decision to do drugs
belongs to the individual.

Our present problems can be solved with faith,
love, hard work, commitment, determination, and
education. If you are armed with these things,
racism cannot hold you down.

Sure, white supremacy is the source of some of our
problems, but the White man won't make you steal a Black
woman's purse. The White man doesn't come into our neighborhoods at night and write graffiti, argue over 40-ounce
bottles of malt liquor, or pee in our alleys.

You have the power to dream, achieve, grow, develop,
and fly. Your power is greater than white supremacy.

Speak without slang.

Communication is information is power.

1. "Sup Ahkee. What's the 411 on a gizig, 'cause a nigga needs a lil' sumpin- sumpin in his slide?"
2. "Good morning, sir. I'd like some information on possible employment with your company. I'm seeking to provide a better financial base for my family and myself."

If these two statements sound like different languages, it's because they are. Statement #1 might get you a job selling caps on the corner but not a job in corporate America. You'll need to speak standard English (statement #2) for that. Around the world, it is often said that if you speak only one language, you must be American. For Black folks that is not completely true. Most of us can speak standard English as well as our cultural slang. The key is knowing when to use which language.

YO, LITTLE BROTHER

Don't let racial slurs upset you.

Nigger, coon, spear chucker, spade, jigaboo, spook, jungle bunny, and porch monkey are some names you will probably hear at some time in your life. How you react to these vile words is the key to handling negative situations.

Don't respond by calling the offender names like whitey, honky, po' white trash, or pale face. That puts you on their small-minded level. People call you names to hurt you, but don't let their stupidity get you down. Don't give your power away. Remember, identify your emotions, then deal on a mature level. Your ancestors survived a whole lot more.

Laugh at the insult and walk away. When you argue with a fool, people can't tell which one of you is the fool. When two people are shouting, you both look like fools.

Stay calm when confronted with racism. Don't get angry. Remember this axiom: "Anger is one letter away from danger." (Anon.)

If you can't walk away, firmly tell the person that you don't appreciate that type of humor. Don't swing at him unless he swings first.

Don't worry when it seems easier for Black women than you.

Black men will not get the same chances that Black women will. Black men are denied many opportunities for employment. There's an underlying fear that Black men will gain some sort of power and marry White women.

Not only will Black women be hired for their abilities, but for the possibility of sexual favors in the future. This makes it extremely hard on a Black man who is looking for a job.

Would you hire someone you were afraid of? Would you hire someone who is traditionally portrayed as a villain? Would you hire someone who is portrayed as shiftless and lazy? Wouldn't you be afraid of hiring someone you thought wanted your wife, daughter, or mother?

Would you hire someone who might be capable of violence if you fired them? The answer to all of these questions is no.

Don't let it get you down. Keep trying in spite of the odds. Laziness is not a part of your legacy. Your ancestors worked for 400 years for free. Stay determined when all seems lost. Depend on yourself. You will make it.

Speak standard English.

The plural of you is not y'all. It isn't you all, youse, yizz or you guys. The plural of you is you.

Every generation has its own slang. Every cultural group has its own slang. Every section of the country has its own dialect. How many times have you heard a White person call a creek a crick, or an aunt an ant, or said "he goes" instead of "he said?" However, no matter which big city you are in, the announcers on the evening news all speak the same standard English.

If you want a decent, well paying job, learn to speak standard English. Carefully study these do's and don't's of the English language.

Use	Don't Use
I am	I be
Ask	A x
you	y'all
this	dis
that	dat
these	dese
them	dem
those	dos
north	norf
south	souf
east	ease
west	wess
my fault	my bad
I'm getting ready to	Um bout to

Do you know what I mean?	Nawmean?
Do you know what I'm saying?	Naumzayin?
Did you eat?	Jeet?

If you are looking for a job, don't use these words as pronouns: Chumpie, jont, thang, maulvaka (motherfucker), chumpski.

Avoid using the following adjectives: phat, bumpin, chronic, salty, all that, and kickin'.

Avoid saying "Naumzayin" after every phrase. If you are speaking clearly, then they will know what you are saying.

Avoid using the following verbs: skeezin, frontin, bitin, mackin, freakin, sweatin, and pookin. If you need to find out how to speak standard English, listen to newscasters read. They got their jobs by being proficient at standard English.

GUARDING YOUR HEALTH

Leave the drugs alone.

Don't sleep on it.

Why do you think they call it dope, dope? As the director of a drug treatment clinic, I (Jeffrey) work with hundreds of drug addicts on a daily basis. None of these addicts planned to get hooked the first time they used drugs. Most of them were teens when they first started. Hard drugs are appealing to some people because they dull emotional pain.

The media has long made the practice of using drugs appear harmless, normal, even hip. The reality is drug use causes despair, discouragement, poverty, and death.

Even legal drugs are dangerous and deadly. Cigarettes and alcohol are the most widely used drugs and the most costly in terms of money and lives lost or destroyed. Yet, they are both widely available.

It is important to remember that hard narcotic drugs like heroin, cocaine, and pills are painkillers or anesthetics and have medical origins. Crack has become the new form of slavery. People use drugs because they are empty and weak. Get high off life, realize your body is His temple.

Protect your health with your life.

There is no survival without health. Your body is the only thing you can have full power over. Your physical health must always be top priority.

Did you know that Black men live about 8 to 10 years less than all other groups in this country? There is an old saying that goes, "Your health is your wealth." If that's true, then Black men are very poor.

Black men die from hypertension, diabetes, cancer, and violence. Many, if not all of these ailments, are preventable.

Eating right, exercising, sleeping, practicing safe sex, and avoiding stress will give you good health. Take a walk in nature to calm yourself down.

Don't use drugs and don't drink alcohol. Don't get in a car with a drunk driver.

Take your health into your own hands. You have the power and you're worth it.

All young Black men should be tested for sickle cell anemia.

Although it also affects people of Hispanic, Middle Eastern, and Mediterranean origins, one of every 13 Blacks in the United States is born with genes that can lead to sickle cell disease. Sickle cell anemia causes periodic attacks that include severe pain and fever. It can damage body organs.

Sickle shaped cells block the normal flow of blood through the capillaries and keep oxygen from flowing to tissues and organs. This condition leads to the periodic attacks.

Ask your doctor or school nurse about the disease and learn more about it. There are sickle cell associations in many large cities. Make sure you get tested for sickle cell anemia and all of its traits and forms.

You can have the sickle cell trait and never get the disease, but it could be passed on to your children. Sickle cell is a serious life-threatening condition. So, young Black men, beware.

Check your blood pressure.

You should have your blood pressure checked at least twice a year.

There is a large problem with hypertension in African American communities. High blood pressure is the leading cause of heart attacks, strokes, and kidney failure. According to the *World Book Encyclopedia*, "The percentage of African Americans who suffer from hypertension is about twice as large as the percentage of White Americans who have it."

Obesity, stress, smoking, and eating too much salt not only can trigger hypertension in people who inherit such a tendency, but they can make a bad situation worse.

Often, people with high blood pressure show no symptoms. Without any warning, an artery in the brain can burst, which causes a stroke. Restricted blood flow to the kidneys can cause kidney failure.

Don't think it cannot happen to you. Several African American basketball players at the high school, collegiate, and professional levels have died from this disease. Have your blood pressure checked frequently. If you are overweight, go on a diet. Avoid salty foods and start an exercise program.

Dress for the weather.

Throughout all my years as a teacher, I (Anthony) have seen young brothers who wouldn't dress appropriately for the weather. They come to school in the rain and snow with their heads uncovered. I've seen young brothers wearing sneakers in the snow.

Some students who claimed they didn't have hats or boots had $100 sneakers. The problem was that they had no priorities. They didn't think a season ahead. Instead of buying a pair of $100 sneakers, they should have bought a $50 pair. Then they could have afforded to get a pair of $40 boots, a $5 hat, and a $5 pair of gloves. Dress appropriately for the weather if you want to survive.

Practice safe sex.

As a young Black person in America, your chance of contracting AIDS is higher than any other age group. The problem is that you think it can only happen to someone else.

Even after hearing Magic Johnson talk about how his life-style led to his HIV infection, many brothers still refuse to practice safe sex. Too many young brothers think that you have to be an addict or gay to get AIDS.

Young Black men today fail to personalize the information. They need to assess the relationships they are in by asking themselves the following questions: Am I prepared to use a condom? Do I know anything about my partner's sexual history? Remember, brother, you sleep with your partner's history, not just her body. Is one sexual encounter worth your life?

IT'S YOUR MONEY

Avoid borrowing and lending.

There's no surer way to lose or damage a friendship than by borrowing or lending money. That's not to say that we shouldn't have people we can count on in a bind, but when that is the case, be diligent and prompt in repaying your debt.

If ever you feel compelled to lend money to someone who is not your trustworthy friend or relative, lend only what you can spare and don't expect your money back. Cut your losses and chalk it up as the cost of discovering this person's real personality. If you're repaid, it will be a pleasant surprise.

When you are able to get credit, use it wisely. Avoid using credit cards to buy merchandise. Use them only for emergencies and restricted required credit card purchases, such as car rentals and ordered items.

Read the newspapers every day and you will see many examples of young Black men hurting each other over money. Don't put other young Black people in a position to become your enemy over money.

Don't lend out your transportation.

A good way to lose a friend is to lend out your car, bike, or school tokens. If the borrower doesn't bring back your wheels or fare on time, you will probably be angry. If they bring it back damaged, you will be steamed. If they lose it, your friendship could end. Lend your things only to responsible people. If you have any doubts about a person, then follow your gut feelings.

Someone could borrow your car, get you a parking ticket, cause an accident, or commit a crime without telling you, then you'd be in a jam. Even when a friend says, "I'll fill up your car," he's not counting the wear and tear he puts on your car, the money you spent on insurance, the cost of repairs, or the inconvenience he causes you.

Get a part-time job.

There is always a way to make a legal buck. Anthony's grandfather used to always say, "I'd shovel horse shit with a spoon before I'd go hungry." What he meant was that you can't be afraid to get your hands dirty to make an honest dollar. Shovel snow, mow lawns, cut hedges, run errands for the elderly, rake leaves, clean basements, paint porches, put up awnings in spring, take awnings down in fall, wash cars, mop floors, pump gas, shine shoes, walk dogs, wash dogs, clean garages, deliver pizza, or wash dishes. Use your imagination. There's always work to be done and someone willing to pay for it. A real man should not depend on welfare or a woman to take care of him.

Stop worrying about designer labels.

Don't judge friends by the brand names on their cloth-ing. You don't need a designer's name on your clothes to look good. As long as your clothes are clean and pressed, you will always look good.

No one is paying you to advertise their product so why go around like a walking billboard? Don't bother your parents for $150 sneakers unless you are headed for the NBA. If you are that good, you'll get your sneakers free anyway.

If you need designer labels to enhance your feelings of self-worth, then you are having problems with your ego. Sure, a new set of clothes will make you feel more confi-dent, but you don't have to spend extra money on a name brand. If you can spend $25 on a good pair of jeans, why spend $100? Companies are banking on you not being a smart consumer. Marketing expensive designer goods to African Americans is one way to keep us in financial trouble. You can't build economic power if all of your money is spent with others.

Cut your parents a break and don't beg for overly expensive clothes. You may not realize it, but your parents' bills can be overwhelming. They have to pay rent or a mort-gage. They have to pay for gas, electricity, telephone, water, the car note, life insurance, house insurance, car insurance, and the food that you eat.

With all of those bills on their backs, they also have to give you allowance, repair the house and car, and save money for the future.

If you want that expensive gear, get a job. Be sure, however, to offer your parents a little money to help with your keep.

If you are a person who wears designer gear, please be careful where you wear it. The newspapers are full of stories of young Black men who were killed for their coats, sneakers, and jewelry. Don't think it can't happen to you.

Forget about the Joneses.

The Temptations said it back in the 70s, "Don't let the Joneses get you down." Just because your friends have something new doesn't mean you need it too. Your car, coat, or sneakers were fine until you saw someone with something newer. So you beat your brains out trying to keep up with them.

Look, if your sneakers don't have holes in them don't sweat it. If your car has a bad paint job and torn upholstery don't worry about it. As long as you keep it clean and it gets you there and back, it's a good car.

When you think you need new shoes, think about the people with no feet. Just because somebody else has it doesn't mean it's to die for. If there's something that you absolutely must have, put it on layaway. Try to tell the difference between what you want and what you need. One of the main problems of young Black men is that they don't know the difference.

Making finding work your job.

If you are an unemployed Black man, spend all of your after school hours looking for a job. Newspaper and radio ads are a good place to start. Buy a Sunday paper on Saturday night and get a jump on the want ads. Get a resume typed regardless of your job history. Put your name, address, and telephone number at the top. Keep it brief. Be honest. Indicate your work experience and education clearly and briefly. Have someone check it for spelling and neatness, then go get 100 copies made, and buy as many postage stamps as you can afford.

Ask two or three teachers, ministers, or some other adults that you respect for their permission to list them as references on your resume. You should also get their addresses and phone numbers.

Now carefully study the employment section of the newspaper. Mail a resume to every job that you qualify for and a couple of jobs that you don't. Look at the heading of each entry and try to picture yourself doing that job. If you can, circle it. If not, skip it and move on. Have fun. Keep an open mind and imagine yourself in your career. Take an hour or two and check the ads from A to Z. While you are circling the companies you want to contact, use the opportunity to think about what kind of career you want to pursue in life. A tour through the want ads is a great way to discover the many varied options the corporate world has to offer.

Know the difference between wants and needs.

You want designer clothes. You need clean clothes. You want a fancy car. You need transportation to get you from point A to point B. You want an expensive stereo system. You need a good radio. You want cable TV, but maybe you need to· read.

Wants and needs are deceiving. You want things that you can live without. You need things to live. Needs are so much more important than wants. Needs take priority over wants.

You may want a certain food, but what you really need is a nourishing meal. You may want a Rolex, but you can have a good watch that tells the same time for a whole lot less. Let's face it, two o'clock is two o'clock whether your watch cost you $50 or $1,000.

I have seen too many young Black men who live in the projects and drive fancy cars. They could probably move to a better neighborhood if they didn't waste so much money.

107

Don't steal.

When we were in college a lot of our friends were thieves. We would justify stealing by not stealing from anyone Black. We were under the false illusion that we weren't hurting anyone but the White man.

We started off by swiping food from local stores and supermarkets. We invoked the "buy one get one free" rule whether it was in effect or not. Soon, we wouldn't even buy one. We knew we weren't going to buy anything when we went into stores because we did not have any money. So we would go in and take what we wanted and leave.

We got good at it. We would share our techniques with groups of other guys who were also shoplifters. Guys had all kinds of techniques. We really thought we were slick, until we got caught.

Eventually, we all got nabbed by the authorities while stealing or shoplifting. Since we were college students, we got a break from the court. But, we all had to pay fines, spend several hours in jail, and face the embarrassment of having to call our parents and school officials to get bailed out. If we had been just some young brothers on the street, the outcome could have been much worse.

We hurt ourselves, and we hurt our community. Our foolishness cost us in time and money, and what's more, we drove up the costs at stores. Back then our attitude was, "So what, we're not buying anyway." But what about the other brothers and sisters who didn't steal? We were hurting them. We might as well have taken money right out of their pockets. When you steal, you hurt everybody. The store owners have to pass the loss to someone. Guess who?

If you look into your heart, most of things you want to steal you don't need. If we had not spent our spare change on frivolous things, we could have pooled our money and bought the things we needed without risking jail, criminal records, or worse.

Learn how to save.

Pay God first by tithing and pay yourself second. Most people define savings as what is left over after spending. This strategy will leave you broke at retirement. Many people who lack discipline have chosen to have their savings deducted automatically from their checking account.

The next step after savings is choosing an investment strategy. If you open a checking account, savings account, certificate of deposit, or money market the banks will guarantee a two to six percent return. Question: If the banks guarantee two to six, might they earn more somewhere else? Where is that? Check out mutual funds, common stock, and real estate. Save at least ten percent and invest your money where the bankers invest their money.

COMMON COURTESY

Don't blast your music in public.

Not everyone over 40 hates rap. I (Anthony) like some of it myself. I like all kinds of music and I'm really not a fan of censorship. Youth must be served. You are entitled to like any kind of music you want. Problems occur, however, when you force music on others by blasting it loudly.

I'm not down on rap. I'm down on any music being forced on me. Jazz, opera, R&B, rock, funk, reggae, or whatever—if it's too loud, you are probably bugging someone. In this era of technology, you don't have to be loud. Do everybody a favor and get yourself a personal cassette player with headphones. No one should have to speak loudly to be heard over your music. Noise is as bad as any other kind of pollution. Some cities even write citations for radios being played too loudly. You might have to pay a fine.

Be sure that you respect everyone's right to a little peace. When folks come home from work they want to relax. It's hard to read the paper, watch TV, or take a nap when someone on your block is blasting their music.

Be considerate of other people if you want them to be considerate of you. The Bible says, "As you sow, you will reap." The Golden Rule is, "Do unto others as you would have them do unto you." In the old neighborhood we used to say, "You get what you bring." No matter how you say it, you are responsible for how you are treated.

Don't walk around rapping aloud to yourself.

If you really want to look crazy, walk around reciting rap lyrics to yourself. To other people on the street you will look like a nut. To them, you are just another person who talks to himself. It doesn't matter how relevant or important you think your words are, if you are not talking to another person you'll seem like another babbling idiot who needs help.

You already have enough problems being a young Black man. Don't make people think you are young, Black, and crazy.

Don't brag.

If you accomplish something good, don't brag about it. You will only make people jealous and resentful of you.

Let your deeds speak for themselves. Actions speak louder than words anyway. Shakespeare once said, "Have more than you show, say less than you know." He had the right idea.

Young brothers love to brag about conquering young sisters. Never kiss and tell. All this does is ruin the reputations of the girls. Give them the same respect you give your female family members.

If your team wins a sport, don't brag too loudly because when you lose it will hurt twice as bad. Be conscious of the other guy.

Go as far as you can in life, then help someone else, but don't be boastful about it. You need all the allies you can get in this life. Don't make enemies out of brothers who could be friends.

Leave things alone that don't belong to you.

If you didn't buy it, it's not yours. If it wasn't a gift to you, it's not yours. If you didn't win it, it's not yours. Leave other people's things alone.

Just because you know someone, doesn't mean you have carte blanche to their belongings. You must always ask permission, whether it's car or a cookie.

The newspapers are full of people hurting other people over seemingly ridiculous items. You never know how much something means to another person so leave other stuff alone. O.P.P. (other people's property) can get you D.O.A. (dead on arrival).

Don't be a gossip.

He say, she say will get you in trouble. Never spread rumors. When you do you become part of a network of misinformation. In the African American community where word is often spread by mouth, gossip really hurts.

As a high school teacher for 18 years, I (Anthony) have heard some doozies. Some were so far fetched they could not possibly be based on reality. Still, they were taken as gospel truth and passed on through the grapevine.

Remember the old game where you sat in a circle and passed a phrase along to the next person? When the words reached the end of the line, their meaning had changed completely. There's an old saying from Buffalo, New York: "The way to make a mountain out of a molehill is to keep on adding dirt."

The more you repeat an untrue rumor, the more it is believed. Whether it is based on fact or fiction, if you weren't there and you didn't see it, how do you know what's true?

If you have a productive life of your own, then you won't have time to waste talking about others.

Don't air dirty laundry.

Don't say negative things about African Americans in front of people of other races. When you call a friend a derogatory name in front of others they will think it's OK to do it too.

"Yo, nigger," "What's up, hoe," "Hey, bitch." Believe it or not, these were girls talking. You can imagine what the boys were saying.

Speak positively about your people. Don't dwell on negativity. There's too much of it to go around.

Let people know that you love being Black. Let people know that you are proud to be part of a people who rose up from slavery.

Practice unity, help each other when you can, and only speak about your brothers to others in the tribe. Like Bob Marley said in "Who the cap fit," "Man-to-man is so unjust, you don't know who to trust." Discuss race with other cultures, but don't put your people down in the process.

Think before you answer questions about controversial African American leaders. Even if you don't agree with some of our self-proclaimed leaders, just hope that their mission is for our betterment. Never give another guy ammunition to shoot you with.

Always address authority figures with respect.

This could be the difference between you being arrested or not. Police officers, judges, probation officers, teachers, parents, and others want to be treated with respect. Refer to them by their last name or their title. Avoid calling an adult by their first name. Keep your conversation positive because you want to appear educated and seem like someone with a future. If your manners are intact you may just get the break you're looking for.

How you act when stopped for questioning will determine how you will be perceived. Remember, you already have one strike against you because you are a minority male. Don't worry about "sounding white." Make sure you speak clearly—your life may depend on it.

If you are ever arrested, stay calm. Follow instructions. Use your phone call wisely; you will probably only get one. Call your parents. They will know what to do better than one of your friends.

You've got to give respect to get respect. When you give your elders the proper respect, they will be willing to give you more in return.

Watch your manners.

Always mind your manners. Open doors for women. Give up your seat for elders and women. Say "thank you," "no, thank you," "please," "excuse me," "sir," and "ma'am." These words are keys to your getting treated respectfully.

You can go a whole lot further in life with manners than without them. Manners separate a civilized society from an uncivilized one. If you show no manners to other people, none will be shown to you.

Let people think that you came from a decent home, whether you did or not. A man with no manners is considered a jerk with no class. He won't go far. As a young African American male, you need to exhibit the best manners possible. Many people expect less of you. Prove them wrong.

Be sensitive to the needs of other people.

It doesn't hurt to be sensitive. You're not a punk if you care. Caring about others is a sign of maturity. Young brothers who don't care about other people aren't being true to themselves or the rest of mankind.

I (Anthony) had to straighten out my 16-year-old son after the death of Bill Cosby's son, Ennis. He said, "Just because he's famous everybody's getting all worked up over him." I told him that was not the case. We get worked up over the death of any young person. If we don't care about others, how can anybody care about us?

When Ennis was killed, that was one more young Black person dead. We need to be concerned about that. We need all the successful young Black role models we can find. The death of this young man who was working on his Ph.D. is not only a blow to our community but to the world.

We do not respect life anymore. Life has become a cheap thing. Life has become something that we can snuff out easily. When it happens to the other guy, we turn a blind eye and deaf ear to it.

I don't know what happened to make our youth so insensitive. I don't know what makes our youth think they have to be so cold, but they seem to think being hard is a method of survival. You may survive, but you'll miss much of the joy of living. Care about people. Care about the world.

Always ask the prettiest girl at the party to dance.

I (Jeff) was painfully shy as a boy. In my neighborhood we had red light basement parties every weekend. While everyone was jammin' to James Brown or slow draggin' to Smokey and the Miracles, I spent a lot of time against the wall because I was too shy to ask a girl to dance. I was afraid of rejection. Eventually, I gained confidence.

By high school I created my own rule that not only eliminated my feelings of "punkdom" but increased my success rate with the nice girls I liked. I always made it a point to ask the prettiest girl at the party to dance.

If there are two pretty girls at the party, then ask them both to dance. I look for the Pam Grier, Toni Braxton, Vanessa Williams, or Tyra Banks. Give her a big smile, and then ask her to jam. You know she's gonna turn you down anyway, so what's the difference? Everyone will be peeping at her and if you get rejected the fellas will say you have heart. The rest of the ladies will give you that sympathy dance.

But guess what? Very often that fine lady has been sitting there waiting for somebody to approach her. They would say that nobody asked them to dance because they thought they would get rejected. So sometimes I'd get a yes.

When you're dancing with the prettiest girl at the party you really get the respect of the fellas, and the rest of the ladies will like you too.

121

Pass it on.

Do a favor for someone today. It will come back to you. It doesn't have to be anything big. Good things will come to you again at sometime in your life.

Hold the door open for somebody. Speak to an elder. Go to the store for somebody for free. When you sweep your walk, sweep your neighbors' walk too. Fix a bike for a little kid. Let people change lanes when you are driving, and give pedestrians a break. Say a prayer for somebody. Help somebody change a tire. There are a lot of little things you can do to make the world better, and it will in turn treat you better.

Be punctual.

Make it a habit to always be on time for everything. Being on time is not always important, but when it is you'll be ready. Punctuality separates the people who are ready, willing, and able from those who don't care. Many an opportunity has been lost just because someone else was there to grab it first.

A writer once stated that 80% of making something work is showing up. We would add another 10% for punctuality. Being punctual helps to create a positive first impression. Punctuality makes the world run smoothly. Imagine if your bus was always late or if your principal forgot to open the school doors on time. Nothing would get done.

Make sure you don't practice what is called C.P. Time (colored people time). Let the world know that your race built the first calendar and clock. When you're on time, you're also respecting the other person's schedule.

YOUR FUTURE

Find a good role model.

It's easy to just find the most popular persons to emulate. The problem is that many popular people aren't worth emulating.

We have athletes, stars, and politicians who break laws and are involved in all sorts of immoral conduct. These people are often welcomed back into society because of their special talents or fame. They are often forgiven and held in high esteem by the masses.

Make sure your role models are worthy of your adoration. Pick champs, not chumps. Then shoot for the stars. Look at the people in your own neighborhood who work hard every day. Look at your parents or other relatives who struggle against tremendous odds to make it in this world. Look at the large number of African American doctors, lawyers, teachers, cops, firemen, and other professionals who go out daily to "meet the man." They are the true heroes.

YO, LITTLE BROTHER

If you can't enroll in college, find a job, join the military.

If you are between 18 and 21 and you don't have a job or aren't in college, then join the military. Don't sit around the house waiting for you dreams to come true.

For a man with time on his hands, the military could be just the thing to get you on the right track. Sure it could get you killed, but so can hanging in the street.

The military can teach you a trade, get you in physical shape, provide college courses, food, clothing, and shelter for you. In return you get a chance to see the world, and all you have to do is take orders for a couple of years.

Sitting at home will get you nothing. Hanging on the corner will get you in trouble. You say you don't want to take orders from some drill sergeant, professor, or boss? Would you prefer to take orders from some prison guard or your mom because you still live with her? Remember, if you are over 18 there are four major choices available to you—a job, college, the military, or jail.

If you don't have a job or if you're not in college or the service, then you aren't being productive. You aren't helping yourself, your family, or the African American community.

A college degree will open many career doors. The knowledge that you gain is a stepping stone to all things positive.

Going into the military can also be useful as a way of advancing your goals in life. If you choose wisely, military experience can be valuable for a young Black man.

According to retired U.S. Marine Sgt. Bob Michaels, there are at least 10 good reasons why the military can be beneficial to a young Black man:

1. It helps to provide a sense of discipline that is missing in many of our households.
2. It gives you a sense of civic duty.
3. It helps give you a sense of daily order.
4. It prepares you to deal with authority figures.
5. It can give you a sense of belonging. There's no need for you to join a gang or a cult.
6. You can get the chance to travel the world and see how other people live.
7. You can build yourself up physically and mentally.
8. There are excellent benefits for college, employment, and life-long medical care for you and your children.
9. You will get to interact with other people from different races, religions, and socio-cultural backgrounds.
10. It is an excellent alternative to hanging in the hood.

Pursue a realistic dream.

You may be a great playground hoopster, but only a small percentage of good players make the high school team. You may be a great high school player, but only a small percentage of high schoolers make a college team. You may be a great college player, but only a small percentage of the great college players make it to the pros.

If you have the skills, give it a shot. If you don't make the team, don't let it get you down. There are many great things you can become. Play ball, but study hard at something else. A Black doctor is a great man. A Black lawyer, teacher, or businessman is a great thing to become. You won't have to beg for anything if you know plumbing, electrical work, or any other skilled profession.

Just because you are not on TV doesn't mean you aren't a star. You may not become a millionaire, but it's how you spend your time that counts anyway.

We need professional young Black men in our communities. Our communities need help. We need heroes—as many as we can find. That doesn't mean that you have to be famous to help. Something as simple as cleaning up your block will make you a hero.

Do all that you can to stay off of welfare.

If you are an able-bodied Black man, there is no reason for you to get on welfare. You need to be an independent, tax paying citizen. There are only two choices: tax payer and tax burden.

We're not going to sugarcoat it. Here's the real deal about life on the welfare rolls: You are taking away from the truly needy, those who can't help themselves. Unless you are sickly, homeless, or old, there is no reason for you to accept this form of dependency. The truly needy can't help themselves.

A man should be able to do better. If you can't, then you should start looking at yourself in the mirror because you are the problem. You need to act like a real man and provide for yourself. A man does not live off welfare money, his mother, or his girlfriend.

Get out of the ghetto or clean it up.

If you are living there, you can do one of two things. Either help clean it up or get out. If you live in shabby surroundings, pick up a broom and sweep your steps. Don't wait for the city to do it. Pick up a paint brush or a hammer and nails. Repair your broken windows. Others will follow your lead. Good work is contagious.

If your situation is really bad and you feel like a prisoner in your own home, then do all that you can to leave. The first order for any prisoner of war is to escape. Even if you can only move a few blocks at a time, do it. Give up some of your creature comforts. Don't get cable TV. Get basic telephone service without all of the frills. Sell your car and ride the bus. Don't buy name brand clothing. Shop in the no frills aisles for a while. Stop renting videos for a few months. Iron your own shirts instead of sending them to the cleaners. Keep your thermostat a few degrees lower. Do all that you can to save a few bucks. Then use that money to move again, and keep moving until you get to where you want to go. This plan may sound tough, but not as hard as living a lifetime in the ghetto. You owe it to yourself to have a good home in a safe neighborhood.

Be ready when opportunity knocks.

There are many opportunities available to you because you are Black. Many organizations exist for your benefit. You will find that opportunities for your advancement are plentiful.

Do you need money for college? Do you need help with a substance abuse problem? Do you need someone to talk to? Do you need help getting out of a gang? Do you need financial advice? Do you need legal help? Are you feeling suicidal? There is help specifically for African Americans.

Don't waste time worrying about the problems that you can't seem to solve. All problems can be solved with help from others. If you don't know where to look, ask somebody. Go to the public library. There are books on every topic. Search the Internet.

Share your dreams.

If you keep your dreams to yourself, they probably won't come true. Vocalize your dreams to people who can help you realize them. You never know who can help you if you don't open your mouth. You could be very close to pursuing your dream, but if you keep it to yourself, you might as well be a million miles away.

No one fulfills a dream alone. Everything worthwhile takes some sort of team effort. Every scientist has lab assistants. Every business person has contacts. Every chef has bakers and sauce makers at his side. Every athlete has coaches and trainers. Beside every good man there is a good woman. Beside every good woman there should be a good man. Find someone who will help you achieve your goals.

Don't assume that people who have less than you can't help you with your dreams. That old brother who looks like he knows nothing can be the one brother who can help you solve a problem.

You can start by talking to your parents, teachers, ministers, or school guidance counselors. A local business-man or community activist can be a good person to talk to. Choose wisely—successful people are the best sources of information.

If you can't join them, beat them.

Take a lesson from the lives of Tiger Woods, Jackie Robinson, Arthur Ashe, or anyone else who was discriminated against. If you're not permitted to join the club, then start your own. When you become good at your particular game, you'll be sought out.

Tiger Woods was not welcome at many golf courses across America because of his skin color. Still, he practiced his game until he became the best. Now he is welcome everywhere. Black men were not allowed in major league baseball, so they started their own league. When White scouts saw how they fielded, pitched, ran, and batted, they started to think twice about that ban. Once they saw the large crowds that the Negro Leagues drew, they knew that something had to be done. They allowed Jackie Robinson in and everything changed.

Right now, we are economically locked out of hockey and swimming even though we can excel at both. There are only a handful of Black players in the hockey league. Actually, there are only a handful of White Americans in the league because most of the players are Canadian. The rest are from Sweden, Finland, Norway, and other cold climate countries.

Identify what you like and pursue it with passion. Whatever your choice is, if you work hard at it and are persistent, you'll get an opportunity to go as far as your talent will take you. You may not have it as easy as some, but by being determined, you'll get your shot.

Prove them wrong.

The best way to counter stereotypes is to prove them wrong. Be different from what everyone expects. Television says that you're a gun toting, car jacking, drug using loser who doesn't care about anything but designer clothes, sneakers, and sex. Radio stations think you are only interested in one type of music. Radio stations that are geared toward young Black men don't mix up their formats.

If all we were interested in was instant pleasure, we would have died out as a race by now. Look through the history of America. It is filled with Black men who were scientists, inventors, leaders, teachers, soldiers, sailors, builders, fixers, writers, and thinkers. We are in many different professions. There is no one way to describe how we think. We are Democrat, Republican, and in between.

We're not going to tell you that you are all the sons of African Kings and Queens. You may be the distant son of a merchant or farmer. More importantly, Dr. Molefi Asante of Temple University, says, "You are the sons and daughters of those who refused to die."

Your ancestors took a severe beating. Those who were sick on the boat ride here were tossed overboard at the mid point of the journey. This place was called the "Middle Passage." When you hear about the Middle Passage, feel sad. This is where millions of Black people died.

The fact that you are here, alive, and kicking shows that you come from the strongest of the strong. You come from a group that survived the ride across the big ocean. You come from a group that was routinely lynched, beaten, denied hospital care, and jobs. They were denied equal access to restaurants and the major leagues. They were denied the right to vote and they were denied their civil rights. They were jailed, lied on, and stripped of their dignity, and they still survived. They were expected to buckle under and die. They did not. They proved their oppressors wrong. So can you. You are their children.

Don't become a statistic.

You've heard all of the bad statistics about Black men today. You die younger. You won't achieve the educational status of the generation before you. You will fill up the prisons. Your enrollment in certain colleges is shrinking. Black men lead the nation in homicides.

Don't become a bad statistic. Keep your nose out of trouble. Stay away from people and situations that you know are wrong. If you have second thoughts about the people around you, move. If a place gives you an uneasy feeling, get out of that place. If you are anywhere or with anyone who gives you bad vibes, get away from them. Stay with those you know you can trust to stay out of trouble.

Carry your own weight.

From the day you are born until the day you die, you and only you will be accountable for what you accomplish. Don't look for anyone else to handle your responsibilities or you will be disappointed.

No one can study for you. No one can give you pride. No one can give you self-determination. No one can give you inner peace. These are things that must come from within.

Once you reach young manhood, don't expect anyone to clothe or feed you. No matter how difficult it seems, being responsible for yourself is the only way you can truly feel good about yourself.

137

Persistence beats resistance.

Barnett Wright, assistant managing editor of the Philadelphia Tribune, came up with this phrase, "persistence beats resistance." Remember it. Your ability to persist through adversity will guarantee success. Wright says that all of the Black men he's interviewed over the years have faced obstacles like hurdles and jumped over them. And each one of those Black interviewees had encountered some sort of racism while trying to succeed.

Many let the setbacks stop them, many went beyond them. The difference between the two groups was their ability to persist. Persistence is dogged determination. Persistence is getting back up when you are knocked down. Persistence is trying one more time, failing, and then trying again.

Resistance, on the other hand, is that wall, that block, that trap, that person who says you can't succeed. Overcome them by gritting your teeth and trying harder. Use the same technique that you use in sports. If someone blocks your shot, do you stop shooting for the rest of the game? If you strike out, do you quit before your next time at bat? If you quit, you lose. Game over.

SEXUALLY SPEAKING

Use protection if you are sexually active.

HIV, syphilis, herpes, gonorrhea, and other STD's should be enough to scare you. Unwanted pregnancies will hinder your chances of survival. Abortions often leave young sisters with feelings of guilt and this can end your relationship.

God provides the best advice: abstinence before marriage. Yet, some teenagers will have sex no matter what, so please, at the very least, practice safe sex. Don't have a baby until you are mature and prepared to provide for your child. Don't lie to a woman and tell her you love her to get sex.

Don't let your testosterone level get you in trouble. Think with your big head, not your little one. If you think it's rough being a young Black man, think of how much tougher it will be with a child to raise. Manhood is not based on the quantity of children you produce, but more the quality that you provide as a father.

If a girl says no—stop!

What part of *no* do you not understand? If you continue after a girl says no, consider yourself a rapist. Even if you think that the girl led you on, it's still rape. If you gave her a night on the town, bought her a great birthday present, or took her to the prom, if she says no, don't force yourself on her. This is the essence of rape. If going to jail for rape can happen to a guy like Mike Tyson with all his money, it can definitely happen to you, especially if you are Black.

Young men are being accused of sexual harassment because of their comments to young women. Some even lose their jobs. Even the President of the United States is not exempt.

It's about respecting women. Don't make comments to a woman that you would not want a man making to your mom, sister, aunt, or daughter.

Don't get in on the train.

Why would you want to be in a group that pulls a train on a girl? What's the matter? Can't you find a girl of your own? Scared the boys will call you a punk? Afraid they'll think you are weak?

You should be afraid of AIDS. What you should be worried about is destroying a girl's future. You should be concerned about what her father, brother, uncle, husband, or boyfriend will do to you when they find out. Pulling a train is gang rape. Be strong enough to stop your associates from acting like animals.

I've never been able to understand how a man can insert his penis into a vagina full of another man's semen. Even if the sex is consensual, the girl could change her mind the next day and then you are in trouble. This type of thing is boasted about in rap music all the time. Getting involved could land you in jail and you could also become the victim of a train.

Take care in choosing a girlfriend.

There's little doubt that after puberty, the desire for a relationship is the most important thing on a young man's mind. That's completely normal. Women are foremost in an old man's mind too.

The key to success in choosing a girlfriend is to know, accept, and understand yourself. This leads to self-love and paves the way to knowing and understanding what is best for you in a relationship. Look for a girl you respect and with whom you share common values, trust, worthiness, honest communication, and mutual interests. It's more important to develop positive, meaningful friendships than it is to become involved in a serious relationship before you're ready.

YO, LITTLE BROTHER

Respect women like you respect your mother.

You don't call your mother a skeezer. You don't call your grandmother a bitch or a whore. You don't want to hear anyone talk about having sex with your mom. You don't want to hear anyone talking about your mom's body parts. If you did, you'd be mad as hell. You would be ready to fight.

Remember, every young woman that you treat poorly is someone's child. I don't care if she has been brainwashed into thinking that she isn't much, you still should treat her with respect. Some young girls think they need to act the way women act in music videos. It's up to you to let them know that they don't. Always be a gentlemen. Your mom would like that. It's not about them being ladies, it's about you being a gentleman.

Take care of your children.

If you didn't follow the advice to abstain or wear a condom and you find that you are a young father, don't panic. Accept the responsibility like a man. Do all that you can to support the mother and the child. If you don't help and you are not there for your child, you are starting a new generation of Black people with problems.

Making a baby does not make you a man, especially if you can't take care of a child.

1. If you make a baby, you have to make a commitment to become emotionally involved.
2. Don't put young Black women in a tragic cycle of struggling alone to raise a child.
3. Don't feel that you can't help. You don't know what you can do until you try. Make an honest effort.
4. Spend some quality time with your child.
5. You can break up with the mother, but you should never depart from your children.

BIBLIOGRAPHY

Famous Black Quotations. Janet Cheatham Bell, Warner Books, New York, NY, 1994.

African American Wisdom. Reginald McKnight, New World Library, San Rafael, CA, 1992.

"Another Day, Another Humiliation." Arnold Rampersad. *New York Times Book Review.* January 9, 1994. Review of Ellis Cose's, "The Rape of the Priviledged Class."

To Be Popular or Smart: The Black Peer Group. Jawanza Kunjufu, African American Images, Chicago, IL, 1988.

Surviving Adolescence or Growing up Oughta Be Easier Than This. Jim Burns, Word Publishing, Dallas, TX, 1990.

Nurturing Young Black Males, Ronald Mincy. Urban Institute Press, Washington, DC, 1984.

African Proverbs. Charlotte and Wolf Success. Peter Pauper Press, Inc., White Plains, NY, 1996.

Daily Motivations for African American Success. Ballentine Books, A Division of Random House, Inc., NY, 1993.

Race Matters. Cornell West, Beacon Press, Boston, MA, 1993.

"The Gun Culture." The MEE Report Update. Issues Of Importance to Urban Youth Service Providers. Philadelphia, PA, October, 1993.

"Reaching the Hip Hop Generation." MEE Final Symposium Report. Philadelphia, PA, May, 1993.

How to Succeed in Business Without Being White. Earl Graves, Harper Collins Publishers Inc., NY, 1997.

Life's Little Instruction Book. H. Jackson Brown, Jr., Ruthledge Hill Press, Nashville, TN, 1992.

Black Child, White Child. Judith Porter, Harvard University Press, 1971.

Straight Up! - A Teenager's Guide to Taking Charge of Your Life. Elizabeth Taylor-Gerdes, Lindsey Publishing Inc., Chicago, IL, 1994.

Minority Organizations - A National Directory Fifth Edition. Ferguson Publishing Company, Chicago, IL, 1997.

"A bleak indictment of the inner-city." (1990, March 12) *U.S. News and World Reports*, p. 14.

"The Evolution of Human Psychology for African Americans." Akbar, N., In Jones, R.L., ed., <u>Black Psychology,</u> Berkely, CA. Cobb & Henry Publishers, 1988.

"Putting Africa at the center." Asante, M.K., *Newsweek*, (1991, Sept. 23).

"Black Caucus tackles crime." Berkman, H., *The National Law Journal*, (1994).

The Measure of our Success. Edelman, M. W. Boston: Beacon. Ferrell, C., (1992).

"The Oudunde African American Festival, its root and relations." Fernandez, L. *Philadelphia Folklore Project: Works in Progress, 6.* p. 2, (1993).

"Deglamorizing street style." George, N. *Essence.* v. 24, p. 174. (1993, Nov.).

"African American strengths: a survey of empirical findings" In R. L. Jones (Ed), *Black Psychology.* (pp. 379-395). Hayles, Jr., V.R. Cobb and Henry Berkeley, CA. (1991).

"Extended self: rethinking the so-called Negro self-concept." In R. L. Jones (Ed), *Black Psychology.* (pp. 295-303). Nobles, W. W., Berkeley, CA: Cobb and Henry, (1988).

"Rescuing the black male." *The Futurist.* (1992, Sept.-Oct.).

"Preparing young leadership." Scales, A. *Emerge.* v. 5, p. 82. (1994, Feb.).

"Afrocentric schools: fighting a racist legacy." Touch, T., *U.S. News and World Reports*, v. 11, p. 74. (1991, Dec. 9).

The Isis Papers: The Keys to the Colors. Welsing, F. Chicago, Third World Press, (1991).

NOTES

NOTES

NOTES

NOTES

NOTES

NOTES

NOTES

NOTES

NOTES